英語教育史
重要文献集成

[監修・解題] 江利川 春雄

■第 1 巻■ 小学校英語

◆ *The Mombushō English Readers for Elementary Schools*
　（小学校用文部省英語読本）　文部省 著
◆ 小学校用文部省英語読本巻一教授書
　文部省 著

ゆまに書房

凡　例

一、「英語教育史重要文献集成」第1期全5巻は、日本の英語教育史において欠くことのできない重要文献のうち、特に今日的な示唆に富むものを精選して復刻したものである。いずれも国立国会図書館デジタルコレクションで電子化されておらず、復刻版もなく、所蔵する図書館も僅少で、閲覧が困難な文献である。

第1巻　小学校英語
第2巻　英語教授法一
第3巻　英語教授法二
第4巻　英語教授法三
第5巻　英語教育史研究

一、復刻にあたっては、歴史資料的価値を尊重して原文のままとした。ただし、寸法については適宜縮小した。

一、底本の印刷状態や保存状態等の理由により、一部判読が困難な箇所がある。

一、第1巻は、今後の小学校英語教育のあり方を考える上で重要な文部省著作の小学校用国定英語教科書と、それに準拠した懇切丁寧な教師用指導書を復刻する。

・文部省著 *The Mombushō English Readers for Elementary Schools*（小学校用文部省英語読本）全3巻、国定教科書共同販売所発行（1930年以降は大日本図書株式会社発行）。第1巻は1908（明治41）年3月19日発行、第2巻は1909（明治42）年3月30日発行、第3巻は1910（明治43）年4月23日発行。

・文部省著『小学校用文部省英語読本巻一教授書』国定教科書共同販売所、1909（明治42）年11月19日発行。

一、本巻の復刻にあたって、読本編纂方針に関する資料を提供された竹中龍範教

授（香川大学）、複写等で協力をいただいた上野舞斗氏（和歌山大学大学院生）に感謝申し上げる。

小学校英語　目次

文部省 *The Mombushō English Readers for Elementary Schools*　第1巻

文部省 *The Mombushō English Readers for Elementary Schools*　第2巻

文部省 *The Mombushō English Readers for Elementary Schools*　第3巻

文部省『小学校用文部省英語読本巻一教授書』

解題　　　江利川 春雄

The Mombushō English Readers for Elementary Schools

THE MOMBUSHŌ ENGLISH READERS

FOR

ELEMENTARY SCHOOLS

No. 1

AN
ENGLISH-JAPANESE
DICTIONARY
FOR UES IN
ELEMENTARY SCHOOLS.

小學字引
英語讀本

（一之卷）　（二之卷）

定價各拾貳錢

本書は文部省英語讀本を初め小學校にて最も必要なる英語を集め皆様に至極譯り易き樣に飜譯したる字引であります學校で英語を學びたるを家庭にて複習する時に最も必要なる書籍であります英語は同盟國の語で世界各國の通用語でありますから大ひに勉強せねばなりません

發行所

松村文海堂

大阪市心齋橋筋一丁目
電話南九番　振替大阪四三二番

販賣所

全國到る處之書店にあり

THE
MOMBUSHŌ
ENGLISH READERS

FOR

ELEMENTARY SCHOOLS

No. 1

KOKUTEIKYŌKASHO KYŌDŌHANBAISHO

TŌKYŌ AND ŌSAKA

LESSON I.

P, A, e, n, p, Ȧ, pĕn.

1. Pen.
2. A pen

WRITING.

A pen.

LESSON II.

B, o, k, a, d, b, ănd, bŏok.

1. Book.
2. A pen and a book.
3. A book and a pen.

WRITING.

A pen and a book.

LESSON III.

I, Y, s, t, i, g, ĭt, ĭs̬, bĭg, Yĕs.

1. It is a book.

2. Is it a big book?

3. Yes, it is a big book.

WRITING.

It is a big book.

LESSON IV.

T, D, h, y, u, the, ŏn, dĕsk, do͞o(do͞o), yo͞u(yo͞o), sēĕ, Ī.

1. The book is on the desk.
2. Do you see the book?
3. Yes, I see it on the desk.
4. I see the desk and the book.

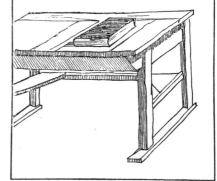

WRITING.

Yes, I see the book on the desk.

LESSON V.

N, W, l, thĭs, nō, nŏt, whạt(whŏt), tāblẹ, thăt, bŭt.

1. Is this a desk?
2. No, it is not a desk.
3. What is it?
4. It is a table.
5. That is a desk, but this is a table.

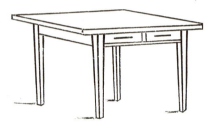

WRITING.

No. That is not a desk, but a table.

LESSON VI.

REVIEW.

Capital Letters.

A, B, D, I, N, P, T, W, Y.

Small Letters.

a, b, d, e, g, h, i, k, l, n, o,
p, s, t, u, y.

Vowel Sounds.

ȧ, ă, ĕ, ĭ, ŏ, ŭ, o͞o, o͝o, ā, ē,
ī, ō.

Consonant Sounds.

b, d, g, k, l, n, p, s, t, y, z,
wh, th.

WORDS.

a,	and,	big,	book,
but,	desk,	do,	I,
it,	is,	no,	not,

on,   pen,   see,   table,
that,   the,   this,   what,
yes,   you.

1. What is on the table?
2. A pen is on the table.
3. Is that a book?
4. Yes. That is a big book.
5. Do you see the desk?
6. Yes, I see the desk.
7. That is not a table, but a desk.
8. Is it not a big desk?

WRITING.

Do you see a book on the big table?

LESSON VII.

H, C, r, c, m, w, hērĕ, lĭt′tlĕ, châịr, thêrĕ(thâr), bĕnch, căn, māỵ, sĭt, down(doun), thănk.

1. Here is a little chair.
2. There is a little bench.
3. Can you see the chair?
4. Yes, I can see it.
5. You may sit down on it.

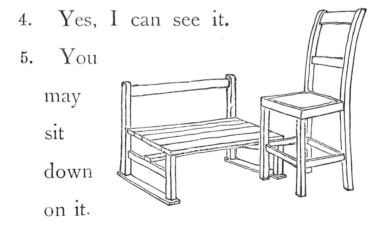

6. Thank you.

8

SPELLING.

ben, den, ken, pen, sen, ten.

WRITING.

Can you sit down on the chair?

LESSON VIII.

M, whĭch, yọur(yōor), pĕn′çĭl(pĕn′sĭl), ĭṣnt(ĭznt), mȳ(mī), ĭn, băg, ẉhọṣe(ẉhōōs), yọurs(yōors), mīnẹ.

1. Which is your pencil?

2. This is my pencil.

3. Isn't this your pencil?
4. No. That is not my pencil.
5. My pencil is in the bag.

6. Whose bag is it?
7. Is it yours?
8. Yes, it is mine.

SPELLING.

it, bit, chit, pit, sit, tit.

WRITING.

My pencil is not in the bag.

LESSON IX.

f, ăn, ĭnk′stănd, fĭnd,
sȯmė(sŭm), ĭnk, blăck,
ôr(ạr), rĕd.

1. What is on the desk?
2. An inkstand is on the desk.
3. What do you find in the inkstand?
4. I find some ink in it.
5. Is that ink black or red?

6. It is black.

7. Is it not red ink?

8. No, it is not red ink.

SPELLING.

bo,   go,   ho,   lo,   no,

so.

WRITING.

What do you find in the inkstand? I find some black ink in it.

LESSON X.

J, O, R, v, j, q, hăvĕ, căp, tōō, hăt, Jŏhn's, Ō, Roy's(rois), hĭṣ, jŭst, līkĕ, ärĕ, quītĕ(kwīt), rīghṭ.

1. Have you a cap?
2. Yes, I have a cap.
3. Is this a cap too?
4. No, it is not a cap, but a hat.
5. Is this John's cap?
6. O, no! It is Roy's cap.

7. His cap is just like mine.

8. You are quite right.

SPELLING.

bat,   cat,   fat,   hat,   mat,

pat,   rat,   sat,

WRITING.

Have you Roy's cap? O, no!

I have John's cap.

It is just like mine.

LESSON XI.

F, x, whêre(whâr), pĕn′knīfe, mŭst, bē, bŏx, plēa̤ṣe, shōw, mē, Frănk's, new(nū), ōld.

1. Where is your penknife?

2. My penknife must be in that box.

3. No, it is not in this box.

4. Please show me the box.

5. Whose penknife is this?

6. It is Frank's.

7. This must be a new penknife.

8. No, it is an old penknife.

SPELLING.

book, cook, hook, look,

nook, rook, took.

WRITING.

Frank's penknife must be in that box. You are quite right.

LESSON XII.

REVIEW.

Capital Letters.

A, B, C, D, F, H, I, J, M,
N, O, P, R, T, W, Y.

Small Letters.

a, b, c, d, e, f, g, h, i, j,
k, l, m, n, o, p, q, r, s, t,
u, v, w, x, y.

Vowel Sounds.

a̤, ä, ȧ, ă, ĕ, ĭ, ŏ, ŭ, ōō,
o̮o̮, â, ā, ē, ī, ō, ū, oi, ou.

Consonant Sounds.

b, d, f, g, h, j, k, l, m, n,
p, r(initial), r(final), s, t, v,
x, y, z, qu, wh, th, **th**, ch.

WORDS.

a,	an,	and,	are,
bag,	be,	bench,	big,
black,	book,	box,	but,
can,	cap,	chair,	desk,
do,	down,	find,	Frank's,
hat,	have,	here,	his,
I,	in,	ink,	inkstand,
is,	isn't,	it,	John's,
just,	like,	little,	may,
me,	mine,	must,	my,
new,	no,	not,	O,
old,	on,	or,	pen,
pencil,	penknife,	please,	quite,

red,   right,   Roy's,   see,

show,   sit,   some,   table,

thank,   that,   the,   there,

this,   too,   what,   where,

which,   whose,   yes,   you,

your,   yours.

1. Isn't this a new hat?

2. That is an old hat.

3. Where is your pencil?

4. My pencil must be in the bag.

5. Have you an inkstand?

6. No, I have not.

7. Whose chair is it?

8. Is it yours?

9. No, it is not mine, but Roy's.

10. Isn't it just like John's?

11. Yes, it is; you are right.

SPELLING.

cot, dot, got, hot, jot, lot,
not, pot, rot, sot.
old, bold, cold, fold, gold, hold,
mold, sold, told.

WRITING.

Where is your new hat? It is not here. Have you a pencil? Yes. I have a pencil.

LESSON XIII.

S, V, E, Q, tāke̍, ŭp, pu̍t(poŏt), ō'pe̍n, shŭt, rēa̍d, vĕr'y̆, goŏd, fĭrst(fĕrst), Eng'lĭsh(ĭng'lĭsh), rēa̍'dĕr.

1. Take up your book.
2. Put your book on the desk.
3. Open the book.
4. Shut it.
5. Can you read the book?
6. Yes, I can.

7. Very good.

8. What is this book?

9. This is the First English Reader.

10. Quite right.

SPELLING.

but, cut, gut, hut, nut, rut,
big, dig, fig, gig, pig, rig.

WRITING.

Open your book.
Shut it. This is the
First English Reader.
Quite right. Very
good.

LESSON XIV.

boy(boi), ăm, a̱l'sŏ, gĩrl(gẽrl), hă̱s(hăz), gŭn, hē, proud, of(ŏv), dŏll, shē, fŏnd.

1. Are you a boy?
2. Yes, I am a boy.
3. Are you also a boy?
4. No, I am not a boy.

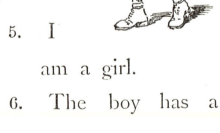

5. I am a girl.
6. The boy has a gun.
7. He is very proud of the gun.

8. The girl has a doll.

9. She is very fond of the doll.

SPELLING.

bake,   cake,   lake,   make,   rake,

sake,   take,   bee,   fee,   see,

deed,   heed,   keel,   meet,   need,

WRITING.

The boy has a gun, but the girl has a doll. Please show me the gun and the doll.

LESSON XV.

L, G, K, U, Z, lŏok, ăt, boys(bois), gĩrls(gẽrls), George(Jarj), hẽr, Kāte, bad, Kĭnzō, Ŭmĕ.

1. Look at the boys and girls.
2. What is your name?
3. My name is George.
4. George is a good name.

5. What is her name?
6. Her name is Kate.
7. Is Kate a bad name?

8. No, it is not a bad name.
9. This boy's name is Kinzō.
10. That girl's name is Ume.

SPELLING.

dew, few, hew, mew, new,
pew, yew, chew.

WRITING.

Boys and girls.
Look at George, Kate,
Kinzō, and Ume.
Kate is a very good
name.

26

LESSON XVI.

X, Z, knōw, ăl'phȧbĕt, ạll,
lĕt'tẽrs, thĕm, smạll, lärg℮,
cạll℮d(kạld), the℘(thā), căp'ĭtȧl,
w̆rīte, thēs℮, thĭnk.

ALPHABET.

Capital Letters.   Small Letters.

A   *A*   a   *a*

B   *B*   b   *b*

C   *C*   c   *c*

D   *D*   d   *d*

E   *E*   e   *e*

F *F*   f *f*

G *G*   g *g*

H *H*   h *h*

I *I*   i *i*

J *J*   j *j*

K *K*   k *k*

L *L*   l *l*

M *M*   m *m*

N *N*   n *n*

28

O	*O*	o	*o*
P	*P*	p	*p*
Q	*Q*	q	*q*
R	*R*	r	*r*
S	*S*	s	*s*
T	*T*	t	*t*
U	*U*	u	*u*
V	*V*	v	*v*
W	*W*	w	*w*

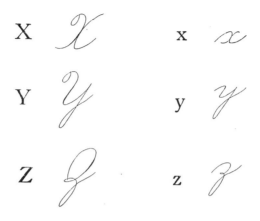

1. Do you know what this is?
2. This is the English alphabet.
3. Can you read all the letters?
4. Yes, I can.
5. Some of them are small letters.
6. Some of them are large letters.
7. What are the large letters called?
8. They are called "Capital Letters."

9. Can you write all these letters?
10. I think I can.

SPELLING.

ink, bink, link, pink, sink, chink, think.

WRITING.

X and Q are new letters. Can you write all the English letters? I think I can. Write them.

LESSON XVII.

stănd, cȯmę(cŭm), whȳ(whī),
gō, tọ(tōō), now(nou), dōọr(dōr),
băck, sēạt, dĭd.

1. Stand up.
2. Stand up and come here.

3. Why do you not stand up?

4. I stand up and go there.

5. Now, you are here.

6. Go to the door.

7. Please open the door.

8. Shut it, please.

9. Go back to your seat.

10. Sit down.

11. Did you sit down?

12. Yes, I did.

SPELLING.

ate, date, fate, gate, hate, late, mate, pate, rate, sate, slate, grate, state.

WRITING.

Why do you not stand up and open the door? Go back to your seat, and sit down.

LESSON XVIII.

REVIEW

Vowel Sounds.

ạ, ä, ȧ, ă, ĕ, ẽ, ĭ, ŏ, ŭ,

o͞o, o͝o, â, ā, ē, ī, ō, ū,

oi, ou.

Consonant Sounds.

b, d, f, g, h, j, k, l, m,

n, p, r(initial), r(final), s, t,

v, x, y, z, wh, th, th, ch,

ng, sh, qu.

WORDS.

a,	all,	alphabet,	also,
am,	an,	and,	are,
at,	back,	bad,	bag,

be,	bench,	big,	black,
book,	box,	boy,	but,
called,	can,	cap,	capital,
chair,	come,	desk,	did,
do,	doll,	door,	down,
English,	find,	first,	fond,
Frank's,	George,	girl,	go,
good,	gun,	has,	hat,
have,	he,	her,	here,
his,	I,	in,	ink,
inkstand,	is,	isn't,	it,
John,	just,	Kate,	Kinzō,
know,	large,	letter,	like,
little,	look,	may,	mine,

36

must,	my,	name,	new,
no,	not,	now,	O,
of,	old,	on,	open,
or,	pen,	pencil,	penknife,
please,	proud,	put,	quite,
read,	reader,	red,	right,
Roy,	seat,	see,	she,
show,	shut,	sit,	small,
some,	stand,	table,	take,
thank,	that,	the,	them,
there,	these,	they,	think,
this,	to,	too,	Ume,
up,	very,	what,	where,
which,	whose,	why,	write,
yes,	you,	your,	yours.

1. Did you open the door?

2. Yes, I did.

3. Who are you?

4. I am Frank.

5. John is a bad boy, but Kate is a good girl.

6. Have you red ink?

7. No, I have black ink.

8. Stand up and read the book.

9. Can you write the alphabet?

10. Yes, I can.

11. What are the Capital Letters?

12. They are the large letters.

SPELLING.

fight,　　　light,　　　might,　　　night,

right,　　　sight,　　　tight,　　　slight.

WRITING.

Can you write the alphabet? Yes, I can. What are the Capital Letters? They are the large letters. Stand up and read the book.

LESSON XIX.

ẉhọ(ẉhōō), waṇt, pā′pẽr, our, tēạch′ẽr, thĭck, thĭn, wē.

1. Who wants this paper?
2. I want it.
3. Whose ink is it?
4. It is our teacher's.

5. Is this your pen, John?
6. No, it is Frank's.
7. This paper is thick, but that paper is thin.

8. Your ink is black, but my ink is red.

9. We have some thick paper and black ink.

10. Our teacher has some thin paper and red ink.

11. May I write on this paper?

12. Yes, you may.

SPELLING.

bow,   cow,   how,   now,   down,

gown,   town,   fair,   hair,   lair,

pair,   chair.

41

WRITING.

John's paper and Frank's ink. The teacher has a pen, but we have pencils. Who wants this paper?

LESSON XX.

fāçe, one(wŭn), mouth, nōṣe,

twọ(tōō), eyes(īs), ēạrs, how(hou),

man'y(mĕn'ĭ), mouthṣ(mouthz), for(fạr),

thĕn, wĭth, hēạr.

1. Look at my face.
2. I have one mouth and one nose.
3. There are two eyes and two ears.
4. How many mouths have you?
5. I have one mouth.
6. How many eyes have I?
7. You have two eyes.
8. What are the eyes for?
9. We see with the eyes.
10. What are the ears for?
11. We hear with the ears.

SPELLING.

boot, cool, doom, fool, loom,

moon, noon, pool, root, soot,

tool.

WRITING.

How many eyes have
you? I have two eyes.
Is my face just like
your face? Yes, it is,
you are quite right.

LESSON XXI.

mādę, wŏod, shọęs(shōos), lĕạth′ẽr, sō, bōots, bōth, gavę, thĭngs, Pȧpä′.

1. What is a desk made of?
2. It is made of wood.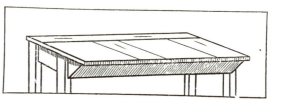
3. What is a book made of?
4. It is made of paper.
5. Is a bench made of wood?
6. Yes, it is.

7. Are shoes made of paper?
8. No, they are not made of paper.
9. What are they made of?
10. They are made of leather.

11. So are boots.
12. Both boots and shoes are made of leather.
13. Who gave you all these things?
14. Papa gave them to me.

SPELLING.

thy, they, that, this, these, those, there, them, then, than.

WRITING.

Both boots and shoes are made of leather. Who gave you all these things? Papa gave them to me.

LESSON XXII.

hănd,   fĭn′gẽr,   tĕn,   fīvĕ,

mōrĕ,   lĕft,   fŏŏt,   fēĕt,

tōĕ,   ēạch,   nāịl.

1. Show me your hands.
2. How many fingers have you?

3. I have ten fingers.
4. Five fingers on the right hand, and five more on the left.

5. This is my right foot.
6. This is my left foot.
7. My feet have five toes each.

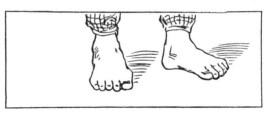

8. Each finger has a nail.
9. Each toe has a nail.
10. Two hands have ten nails.
11. Each foot has five nails.

SPELLING.

thin, think, thick, thatch, theft,
both, pith, tooth, moth, mouth.

WRITING.

How many fingers have you? Five fingers on the right hand, and five more on the left. My feet have five toes each. Each toe has a nail.

LESSON XXIII.

flōor(flōr), wĕll, ĕggs, count,
thrēe, fōur, sĭx, sĕv'ĕn,
eı̆ght(āt), nīne, lĕt, out,
ı̆f, wĭll, lĕft, ōn'lў.

1. What do you see on the floor?
2. I see a box.
3. Very well; and what are there in the box?
4. There are some eggs in it.
5. You are right. Count the eggs.

6. One, two, three, four, five, six, seven, eight, nine, ten. There are ten eggs.

7. Let me take three eggs out of the box.

8. How many are there now?

9. There are seven.

10. If I take three more, how many will be left in the box?

11. Only four.

SPELLING.

are, arm, bark, card, dark, farm, garb, hard, large, park, yard.

WRITING.

One, two, three, four, five, six, seven, eight, nine, ten. There are ten eggs in the box. If I take six eggs out of the box, there will be only four eggs left.

LESSON XXIV.

REVIEW

Vowel Sounds.

a̤, ä, ȧ, ă, ĕ, ẽ, ĭ, ŏ, ŭ,

o͞o, o͝o, â, ā, ē, ī, ō, ū,

oi, ou.

Consonant Sounds.

b, d, f, g, h, j, k, l, m,

n, p, r(initial), r̤(final), s, t,

v, w, x, y, z, wh, th, th,

ch, ng, sh, qu.

WORDS.

a,	all,	alphabet,	also,
am,	an,	and,	are,
at,	back,	bad,	bag,
be,	bench,	big,	black,

book,	boots,	both,	box,
boy,	but,	called,	can,
cap,	capital,	chair,	come,
count,	desk,	did,	do,
doll,	door,	down,	each,
ear,	egg,	eight,	English,
eye,	face,	feet,	find,
finger,	first,	five,	floor,
fond,	foot,	for,	four,
Frank,	gave,	George,	girl,
go,	good,	gun,	hand,
has,	hat,	have,	he,
hear,	her,	here,	his,
how,	I,	if,	in,
ink,	inkstand,	is,	isn't,

it,	John,	just,	Kate,
Kinzō,	know,	large,	leather,
left,	let,	letter,	like,
little,	look,	made,	many,
may,	me,	mine,	more,
mouth,	must,	my,	nail,
name,	new,	nine,	no,
nose,	not,	now,	O,
of,	old,	on,	one,
only,	open,	or,	our,
out,	Papa,	paper,	pen,
pencil,	penknife,	please,	proud,
put,	quite,	read,	reader,
red,	right,	Roy,	seat,
see,	seven,	she,	shoes,
show,	shut,	sit.	six,

small,	so,	some,	stand,
table,	take,	teacher,	ten,
thank,	that,	the,	them,
there,	these,	they,	thick,
thin,	thing,	think,	this,
three,	to,	toe,	too,
two,	Ume,	up,	very,
want,	we,	well,	what,
where,	which,	who,	whose,
why,	will,	with,	wood,
write,	yes,	you,	your,
yours.			

1. Dou you not see many eggs on the table?

2. Yes, I see seven or eight eggs.

3. Show me your fingers.

4. This box is made of wood.

5. Have you my boots?

6. No. Roy has your boots.

7. Whose shoes are these?

8. They are Kate's shoes.

9. Two boys are here, and three girls are there.

10. How many hands have you?

11. I have two hands.

12. Who gave you this paper?

13. Our teacher gave it to me.

14. Let me take up five eggs.

15. If you take two of them, how many will be left in my hand?

SPELLING.

who,   why,   what,   when,

whet,   where,   which,   whip,

whim,   whose,   whom.

WRITING.

Show me your fingers.
This box is made of
wood. I see many eggs
on the table. Let me
take up five of them.
How many more do
you see on the table?

LESSON XXV.

Mā′rў, těll ŭs, sĩr(sẽr), wạtch(wŏch), round, squârę(skwâr), sĭl′vẽr, Hĕn′rў, ĕv′ẽr, bēfōrę′, nĕv′ẽr, sạw, pŏck′ĕt, ŭn′dẽr.

1. Mary, will you tell us what this is?

2. Yes, sir. It is a watch.

3. Is it round or square?

4. It is round.

5. Is this a silver watch?

6. Yes, sir. It is a silver watch.

7. Henry, did you ever see a watch before?

8. No, sir. I never saw one before.

9. Where did I put my watch?

10. You put it in your pocket.

11. Where is it now?

12. It is under the book.

SPELLING.

all, ball, call, fall, gall,

hall, pall, tall, wall, small.

WRITING.

Mary, will you tell us what this is? Yes, sir, it is a silver watch.

Where did I put the watch? You put it under the book.

Henry never saw a watch before.

LESSON XXVI.

bẹạū′tĭfụl(bū′tĭfŏŏl),   flow′er(flou′ẽr),
rōṣẹ(rōz),   whītẹ,   likẹ,   mŭch,
ȯth′ẽr(ŭ-th′ẽr),   Mȧmmä′,   bĕt′tẽr,
thăn,   ȯblīġ′ẹd,   bĕcạụṣẹ′(bĕkạz′),
smĕlḷ,   swēẹt.

1. What a beautiful flower it is!
2. Do you know the name of this flower?

3. Yes, sir. It is a rose.

4. Is this a white rose. or a red rose?

5. It is a red rose.

6. How do you like the rose?

7. I like the rose very much.

8. Mamma likes the rose better than any other flower.

9. You may take this to your Mamma.

10. I am very much obliged to you.

11. Why do you like the rose?

12. Because it smells so sweet.

SPELLING.

her,   fern,   germ,   jerk,   pert,

term,   verb,   sir,   bird,   dirt,

firm,   girl.

WRITING.

What a beautiful flower it is! How do you like the rose? I like the rose better than any other flower. Why? Because it smells so sweet.

LESSON XXVII.

Tàrō, bàs′kĕt, few(fū), ăp′plĕ,
gō′ĭng, ŭn′clĕ(ŭnkl), gĭvĕ, hĭm,
Hànà, ŏr′ängĕ, äŭnt(änt),
wạs(wŏz), kīnd, enough(ĭnŭf′),
ēạt, yọŭrsĕlf′, brŏth′ēr(brŭth′er),
Jĭrō.

1. Tarō, what have you in the basket?

2. I have a few apples in it.

3. What are you going to do with them?

4. I am going to take them to my uncle.

5. Are you going to give him all these apples?
6. Yes, I am.
7. Hana, what have you in the hand?
8. I have an orange.
9. Who gave it to you?

10. My aunt was kind enough to give it to me.
11. Are you going to eat it yourself?
12. No. I am going to give it to my little brother Jirō.
13. Isn't Tarō a good boy?
14. Isn't Hana very kind?

SPELLING.

oil, boil, coil, foil, soil, toil,
coin, join, loin, void.

WRITING.

What are you going to do with these apples? I am going to take them to my uncle. My aunt was kind enough to give me this orange. Are you going to eat it yourself? O, no!

LESSON XXVIII.

môrn′ĭng(mạrn′ĭng), Chärlęs, Lū′çў,
been(bĭn), plāy′-ground, wẽrę,
housę, plāy, fȧst, rŭn, tīręd,
ĭn′tǫ(ĭn′tōo), sĭs′tẽr.

1. Good morning, Charles.

2. Good morning, Lucy.

3. Where have you been?

4. I have been out in the play-ground.

5. Were there many boys and girls there?

6. Yes, there were.

7. I was in the house this morning, and did not play.

8. Let us go out and play.

9. All right.

10. How fast you run!

11. You run very fast.

12. I can not run so fast as you do.

13. I am tired.

14. Let us go into the house.

15. I see your sister there.

SPELLING.

ask, bask, cask, mask, task, cast,

fast, last, mast, past, vast, gasp.

WRITING.

Good morning,
Charles. Where have
you been? I have
been out in the play-
ground. I was in the
house and did not play.
I can not run so fast
as you do.

LESSON XXIX.

Mr.(mĭs′tẽr), Nĭshĭmụrȧ, lŏng, lẽạn′ĭng, yēạr, whĕn, fĭn′ĭsh, shăll, nĕxt, wēẹk, ēlĕv′ẹn, twĕlvẹ, ōld′ẽr, yọŭng′ẽr, thîr′tēẹn(thẽr′tēn), twĕn′tў-sĭx.

1. What is the name of your teacher?
2. Mr. Nishimura is his name.
3. How long have you been learning English?

4. I have been learning English for a year.

5. What have you been reading?

6. I have been reading the First Reader.

7. When will you finish it?

8. I shall finish it next week.

9. How old are you?

10. I am eleven years old.

11. John is twelve, isn't he?

12. Yes, he is a year older than I am.

13. I am two years younger than Mary.

14. Then, Mary is thirteen years old.

15. How many letters are there in the English alphabet?

16. There are twenty six letters in the English alphabet.

SPELLING.

bay, day, gay, hay, lay, may,

pay, ray, say, way, clay, gray,

play, slay, stay, tray.

WRITING.

I have been learning English for a year. We have just finished the First Reader. John is twelve years old, isn't he? Yes, he is a year older than I am. There are twenty six letters in the English alphabet.

LESSON XXX.

REVIEW

WORDS.

a,	all,	alphabet,	also,
am,	an,	and,	apple,
are,	at,	aunt,	back,
bad,	bag,	basket,	be,
beautiful,	because,	been,	before,
bench,	better,	big,	black,
book,	boots,	both,	box,
boy,	brother,	but,	called,
can,	cap,	capital,	chair,
Charles,	come,	count,	desk,
did,	do,	doll,	door,
down,	each,	ear,	eat,
egg,	eight,	eleven,	English,
enough,	ever,	eye,	face,
fast,	feet,	few,	find,

finger,	finish,	first,	five,
floor,	flower,	fond,	foot,
for,	four,	Frank,	gave,
George,	girl,	give,	go,
going,	good,	gun,	Hana,
hand,	has,	hat,	have,
he,	hear,	Henry,	her,
here,	him,	his,	house,
how,	I,	if,	in,
ink,	inkstand,	into,	is,
isn't,	it,	Jirō,	John,
just,	Kate,	kind,	Kinzō,
know,	large,	learning,	leather,
left,	let,	letter,	like,
little,	long,	look,	Lucy,
made,	Mamma,	many,	Mary,
may,	me,	mine,	Mr.

more, morning, mouth, much,

must, my, nail, name,

never, new, next, nine,

Nishimura, no, nose, not,

now, O, obliged, of,

old, older, on, or, one,

only, open, orange, other,

our, out, Papa, paper,

pen, pencil, penknife, play,

play-ground, please, pocket,

proud, put, quite, read,

reader, red, right, rose,

round, Roy, run, saw,

seat, see, seven, shall,

she, shoes, show, shut,

silver, sir, sister, sit,

six, small, smell, so,

some,	square,	stand,	sweet,
table,	take,	Tarō,	teacher,
tell,	ten,	than,	thank,
that,	the,	them,	there,
these,	they,	thick,	thin,
thing,	think,	thirteen,	this,
three,	tired,	to,	toe,
too,	twelve,	twenty-six,	two,
Ume,	uncle,	under,	up,
us,	very,	want,	was,
watch,	we,	week,	well,
were,	what,	when,	where,
which,	white,	who,	whose,
why,	will,	with,	wood,
write,	year,	yes,	you,
younger,	your,	yours,	yourself.

1. Where did you put that silver watch?

2. I put it in my pocket.

3. Did you ever read an English book?

4. Yes, I have just finished the First Reader.

5. Will you take some of these apples?

6. Thank you very much.

7. Do you know the name of this flower?

8. Yes, I know. It is a rose.

9. How many eggs are there?

10. There are eight eggs.

11. Put six of them in this box.

12. Let us go out to the play-ground.

13. I can not go out to play.

14. You may go into the house now.

15. Whose shoes are these?

16. They are Mary's shoes.

17. These shoes are very large, are they not?

18. How many letters are there in the English alphabet?

19. There are twenty six.

20. Very well. You may take your seat.

SPELLING.

nether,   tether,   leather,   feather,

weather,   whether,   gather,   rather,

bother,   mother,   brother.

WRITING.

Tarō is two years older than Jirō. Mary is three years younger than Charles. Henry has a basket of apples. Lucy is going to eat an orange. Papa and Mamma are so fond of roses. They are good and kind to me.

a ア	i イ	u ウ	e エ	o オ
ka カ	ki キ	ku ク	ke ケ	ko コ
sa サ	shi シ	su ス	se セ	so ソ
ta タ	chi チ	tsu ツ	te テ	to ト
na ナ	ni ニ	nu ヌ	ne ネ	no ノ
ha ハ	hi ヒ	fu フ	he ヘ	ho ホ
ma マ	mi ミ	mu ム	me メ	mo モ
ya ヤ	(yi) イ	yu ユ	(ye) エ	yo ヨ
ra ラ	ri リ	ru ル	re レ	ro ロ
wa ワ	(wi) ヰ	(wu) ウ	(we) ヱ	wo ヲ
ga ガ	gi ギ	gu グ	ge ゲ	go ゴ
za ザ	ji ジ	zu ズ	ze ゼ	zo ゾ

da	ji	zu	de	do
ダ	ヂ	ヅ	デ	ド
ba	bi	bu	be	bo
バ	ビ	ブ	ベ	ボ
pa	pi	pu	pe	po
パ	ピ	プ	ペ	ポ

---

kya	—	kyu	—	kyo
キャ		キュ		キョ
sha	—	shu	—	sho
シャ		シュ		ショ
cha	—	chu	—	cho
チャ		チュ		チョ
nya	—	nyu	—	nyo
ニャ		ニュ		ニョ
hya	—	hyu	—	hyo
ヒャ		ヒュ		ヒョ
mya	—	myu	—	myo
ミャ		ミュ		ミョ
rya	—	ryu	—	ryo
リャ		リュ		リョ

gya ギャ	—	gyu ギュ	—	gyo ギョ
ja ジャ	—	ju ジュ	—	jo ジョ
ja ヂャ	—	ju ヂュ	—	jo ヂョ
bya ビャ	—	byu ビュ	—	byo ビョ
pya ピャ	—	pyu ピュ	—	pyo ピョ
kwa クヮ	—	—	—	—
gwa グヮ	—	—	—	—
n ン	—	—	—	—

明治四十一年三月十六日印刷
明治四十一年三月十九日發行
明治四十二年二月二十日再版發行
明治四十三年二月十日三版發行
明治四十四年一月二十日四版發行
明治四十五年一月二十日五版發行

リーダー卷壹
定價金拾貳錢

著作權者	文部省
發行者	株式會社國定教科書共同販賣所
	東京市日本橋區新右衛門町十六番地
代表者	大橋新太郎
印刷者	河合辰太郎
	凸版印刷株式會社代表者
	東京市下谷區二長町一番地
印刷所	凸版印刷株式會社
	東京市下谷區二長町一番地

發行所 株式會社國定教科書共同販賣所
東京市日本橋區新右衛門町十六番地

THE MOMBUSHŌ ENGLISH READERS

FOR

ELEMENTARY SCHOOLS

No. 2

THE MOMBUSHŌ ENGLISH READERS

FOR ELEMENTARY SCHOOLS

No. 2

KOKUTEIKYŌKASHO KYŌDŌHANBAISHO

TŌKYŌ AND ŌSAKA

CONTENTS

LESSON		PAGE
I.	The Horse	1
II.	The Boy and a Dog	4
III.	The Girl and a Cat	7
IV.	The School	10
V.	The Sun, the Moon, and the Stars...	14
VI.	Coins	17
VII.	The Flower Garden	21
VIII.	The Bees	25
IX.	Mount Fuji	28
X.	The Bird's Nest	31
XI.	Rain...	35
XII.	The River	39
XIII.	Swimming	43
XIV.	Playing Ball	47
XV.	Fish...	51
XVI.	The Lamp	55

LESSON		PAGE
XVII.	Flags	56
XVIII.	Papa and Mamma	64
XIX.	The Rats	68
XX.	The Wood	73
XXI.	Water and Fire	77
XXII.	The Carriage	82
XXIII.	Fruit	86
XXIV.	Cows	90
XXV.	Snow	95
XXVI.	Monkeys	100
XXVII.	Age	104
XXVIII.	The Sailboat and the Steamboat	108
XXIX.	Colours	112
XXX.	The End of the School Year	117
	Word List	121

LESSON I.

hôrse(hars), fīne, dōn't, făt, sēems,
strŏng, rīde, măn, hôrse'băck,
fä'thẽr.

THE HORSE.

1. Do you know what this is?
2. Yes. It is a horse.
3. What a fine horse he is!
4. Don't you think he is a very fat horse?
5. Yes, I do.
6. He seems to be very strong.

7. Can you ride on a horse?

8. No, not very well.

9. Who is the man on horseback?

10. It is my father.

SPELLING.

dine, fine, kine, line, mine, nine, pine, vine, wine, thine.

EXERCISES.

1. Is _____ your father?

2. Yes, it is _____ father.

3. Do you _____ the man on horseback?

4. No, I do —— know him.

5. —— is a very strong horse.

6. This horse is fat —— strong.

7. Can you ride —— a horse ?

8. Yes, I ——.

WRITING.

*What a fine horse he is!
Don't you think he is a
very fat horse ? Yes, I do.
He seems to be very strong.*

LESSON II.

dŏg, al′wāys, wĭth, gōes, fŏl′lōws, together, speak, cannot, Spot.

THE BOY AND THE DOG.

1. What do you see?
2. I see a boy and a dog.
3. Is the boy fond of the dog?
4. Yes, he is very fond of the dog.
5. Is the dog always with the boy?
6. Yes. When the boy goes out, the dog always follows him.

7. Do they play together?
8. Yes, they do when they are together.
9. Can the dog speak to the boy?

10. No, he cannot.

11. What is his name?

12. His name is Spot.

SPELLING.

cheat, flea, speak, steam, clear, steal,
treat, sneak, spear, squeak, plead, breach.

EXERCISES.

1. The dog can _____ speak.
2. They play when they _____ together.
3. Are you fond _____ the dog?
4. Yes, I am very _____ of the dog.
5. Where _____ the dog?
6. He is under _____ table.
7. Is he _____ large dog?
8. No, he is a _____ dog.
9. What is _____ name?
10. Spot _____ his name.

WRITING.

Is the dog always with the boy? Yes. When the boy goes out, the dog always follows him. The boy is very fond of the dog.

7

LESSON III.

lăp, căt, kĭt′těn, dȯėṣ(dŭz), fēėd, rīçė(rīs), fĭsh.

THE GIRL AND THE CAT.

1. Who is this girl?
2. She is my sister Mary.
3. What has she on her lap?
4. She has a little cat on her lap.
5. A little cat is called a kitten.
6. Does Mary like the kitten better than her doll?
7. Yes, she likes the kitten much better than her doll.

8

8. What does she feed the kitten with?

9. She feeds it with rice and fish.

10. Do you know the name of the kitten ?

11. No, I do not.

SPELLING.

beaten,   bitten,   eaten,   fatten,   kitten,
mitten,   rotten,   smitten,   written.

EXERCISES.

1. Is this ——— sister ?

2. Yes, she ——— my sister.

3. What is ——— name ?

4. Her name ——— Mary.

5. Where is ——— kitten ?

6. It is ——— Mary's lap.

7. She feeds the ———— with rice ———— fish.
8. How does ———— like the kitten ?
9. She likes ———— kitten better ———— her doll.

WRITING.

My sister Mary has a little kitten on her lap. She likes the kitten much better than her doll.

LESSON IV.

school(skōol), brick, about',
hŭn'drĕd, frŏm, fĭf'teen,
min'utes(mĭn'ĭts).

THE SCHOOL.

1. Where are you going?
2. We are going to school.

3. Is this brick house your school?
4. Yes, that is our school.
5. Are there many boys and girls in your school?

6. There are about two hundred boys and as many girls.
7. Well, that is a very large school, isn't it?
8. How long does it take you to come here from your house?
9. About fifteen minutes.
10. That is not very long.

SPELLING.

abound, about, aground, around, along, among, alone, atone, abide, aside, adieu, anew.

EXERCISES.

1. Are they going —— school ?
2. Yes, they are —— to school.
3. What —— that brick house ?

4. That is ―――― school.

5. Is it a large ―― ?

6. No, it is ―――― very large.

7. How many boys ―――― there ?

8. There are about two hundred ―――― .

9. Are ―――― as many girls ?

10. Yes, there ―――― .

WRITING.

There are about two hundred boys and as many girls. Well, that is quite a large school,

13

isn't it?　It takes us about fifteen minutes to come here from our house.

LESSON V.

sŭn,　　rīṣệ(rīz),　　ḡĕt,　　sŭn′rīṣệ,
sómệ′tīmệṣ(sŭm′tīmz), .　àft′ẽr,　mo͞on,
brīḡht′ẽr(brīt′ẽr),　brĭḡht,　stärṣ,　shīnệ,
nīḡht(nīt),　　whīlệ,　　daẙ′tīmệ(dā′tīm).

THE SUN, THE MOON, AND THE STARS.

1. Look at the sunrise.
2. How beautiful it is!
3. Do you always get up before sunrise?
4. Not always; sometimes I get up after sunrise.
5. Is this also the sun?
6. No, sir; it is the moon.

7. Which is the brighter, the sun or the moon?
8. The sun is much brighter than the moon.
9. What are these small bright things?

10. They are the stars. They look small, but some of them are larger than the sun.

11. When do they shine?
12. The stars as well as the moon shine at night, while the sun shines in the daytime.

SPELLING.

bore, core, fore, more, shore, store, snore, door, floor, boar, hoar, roar, soar, before, restore, ignore.

EXERCISES.

1. How beautiful ——— sunrise is!
2. When do you get ——— ?

3. I get up —— sunrise.
4. Which —— the smaller, the sun ——
the moon ?
5. The moon is smaller —— the sun.
6. When —— the moon shine ?
7. The moon shines at ——— .
8. Does the sun —— at night ?
9. No; the sun shines in the ——— .
10. You —— quite right.

WRITING.

We always get up before

sunrise.   The moon is

not so bright as the sun.

The stars as well as the

moon shine at night, while the sun shines in the daytime.

LESSON VI.

coins(koinz), gōld, yĕn, fĭf′tў(fĭf′tĭ), sĕn, coin, nĭck′ĕl(nĭkl), kīnd, cŏp′p̃ĕr(kŏp′ẽr), dĭf′fẽrĕnt, rĭn.

COINS.

1. Can you tell me what these things are?
2. Yes, they are coins.

3. These are gold coins—twenty-yen, ten-yen, and five-yen.

4. Are these also gold coins?

5. No; they are silver coins—fifty-sen and twenty-sen.

6. What are the five-sen coin and the ten-sen coin made of?

7. They are made of nickel.

8. How many kinds of copper coins have we?

9. We have two different kinds of copper coins—one-sen and five-rin.

10. How many rin are there in a sen?

11. There are ten rin in a sen.

12. How many sen make a yen?

13. One hundred sen make a yen.

SPELLING.

city,   pity,   duty,   beauty,   bounty,
county, scanty, twenty.

EXERCISES.

1. Ten rin —— a sen.
2. One —— sen make a yen.
3. How many —— of nickel coins have we?
4. We have two —— kinds of nickel coins.
5. Is a **one-sen** coin —— of nickel?
6. **No;** it is made —— copper.
7. How many —— of silver coins are there?
8. There are **two** kinds —— silver coins.
9. Is there a one-yen —— of gold?
10. No, there is ——.

WRITING.

How many kinds of silver coins have we?

We have two different kinds—fifty-sen **and** twenty-sen. There are ten rin in a sen. One hundred sen make a yen.

LESSON VII.

gär′dẹn(gär′dn), fu̱ll(fo͝ol) pret′ty(prĭt′ĭ),
flowers̱, wa̱y(wā), är̤ẹn't(ärnt), pĭc̣k(pĭk),
fôr(fa̱r), lĭl′ĭe̱s̱(lĭl′ĭz), Mrs.(mĭs′s̱ĭs̱),
Tĕr′rў(tĕr′ĭ), sta̱y(stā).

THE FLOWER GARDEN.

1. Let us go down to the garden and look at the flowers.

2. O the garden is full of pretty flowers.

3. Come this way, Mary. Aren't these roses beautiful?

4. Aren't they? May I not pick some of them?

5. Yes, you may; but what will you do with them?

6. I will take them to my mother, for she is so fond of roses.

7. O you are a good girl.

8. Charles, don't you think these lilies are very pretty?

9. Yes, I do. I will pick some of them for my teacher, Mrs. Terry.

10. Let us go into the house now.

11. Yes, we must not stay out too long.

23

SPELLING.

bower,   cower,   dower,   power,   tower,
flower,   our,   hour,   sour,   flour,
scour.

EXERCISES.

1. Come into the ———— and see the flowers.
2. Which of the flowers do ———— like best ?
3. I ———— the roses best.
4. How ———— you like the lilies ?
5. I like them ———— much.
6. You may ———— any of the flowers here.
7. I ———— pick some roses.
8. Will you take ———— to your mother ?
9. You must ———— stay out too long.
10. Let us ———— into the house.

24

WRITING.

The garden is full of pretty flowers. May I pick some of these beautiful roses? Yes, you may. I will take them to my mother, for she is very fond of flowers.

LESSON VIII.

bee(bē), bus′y(bĭz′ĭ) work(wûrk), cŏllĕct′(kŏlekt′), hŏn′ey(hŭn′ĭ), keep(kēp), bee′hive(bē′hīv), should(shŏŏd), ōh(ō), close(klōs), say(sā), might(mīt), sting, clĕv′ẽr(klĕv′ẽr).

THE BEES.

1. The bees are busy at work.
2. They go from flower to flower and collect honey.
3. Where do they keep their honey?
4. They keep it in the beehive.

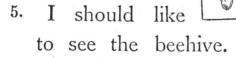

5. I should like to see the beehive.
6. This is the beehive. Oh, you must

not come so close to it.

7. Why do you say so?

8. Because the bees might sting you.

9. The bees are very clever, aren't they?

10. Yes, they are. We have much to learn from them.

SPELLING.

could,   should,   would,   burst,   curse,
durst,   hurl,   lurk,   nurse,   purse,
surge,   turn,   work.

EXERCISES.

1. The bees —— honey from the ——.

2. They keep honey in the ——.

3. Aren't the bees —— clever?

4. Yes, they are. We have —— to learn from them.

5. May I go close ——— the beehive ?
6. No, you must never ——— close to it.
7. The bees might ——— you.
8. They are very busy ——— work.

WRITING.

The bees go from flower to flower and collect honey. They are very clever, aren't they? Yes, they are. We have much to learn from them

LESSON IX.

Mount, Fujĭ, mount′aĭn, bĕlĭevĕ′(bēlēv′),
hīgh′ĕst(hī′ĕst), Jăpăn′, Nĭĭtăkăyămă,
clīmb(klīm), lăst, sŭm′mẽr, rēạch, tŏp,
ŏth′ẽr(ŭth′ẽr), moun′taĭns, hĭll, grănd.

MOUNT FUJI.

1. Is this Mount Fuji?

2. Yes, it is.

3. I believe it is the highest mountain
    in Japan.

4. No; it is
    the second
    highest.

5. Which is
    the highest
    mountain in Japan?

6. The highest mountain in Japan is
    Niitakayama.

7. Did you ever climb Mount Fuji?

8. Yes, I did last summer.

9. When I reached the top of Fuji, the other mountains about it looked like small hills.

10. Did you see the sunrise there?

11. Yes, I did. It was beautiful and grand.

SPELLING.

believe,   relieve,   deceive,   receive,
conceive,   climb,   bomb,   comb,
dumb,   limb,   numb.

EXERCISES.

1. Fuji is the——mountain in Japan, isn't it?

2. No ; the highest——in Japan is Niitakayama.

3. When ——— you climb Fuji?

4. Last ———.

5. Did you _____ the sunrise there?
6. I saw a very _____ sunrise.
7. Did you reach the _____ of Fuji?
8. Yes, _____ did.
9. How did the _____ mountains look?
10. They looked _____ small hills.

WRITING.

When I reached the top of Fuji, the other mountains about it looked like small hills. Did you see the sunrise there? Yes, I did. It was beautiful and grand.

LESSON X.

bĭrd'ṣ, nĕst, trēe͕, sȯme′tīme͕, ȧgō′,
found, tŏŏk, hōme͕, mȯth′ẽr(mŭth′ẽr),
bĭrd, săd, cāme͕, sōōn, yo͝ŭng,
hẽrsĕlf′, lĕsṣ, lȯve͕ṣ(lŭvz), wȧḷk.

THE BIRD'S NEST.

1. Do you see a bird's nest in that tree?

2. Yes, I do. I think there must be some eggs in it.

3. Let us climb up the tree and take the eggs.

4. O no! We must not take them.

5. Sometime ago when John and I found a bird's nest, we took all the eggs home.

6. The mother bird must have been very sad when she came back to her nest.

7. Does a mother bird think so much of her eggs?

8. Yes, she does. They will soon be birds like herself.

9. I did not know that.

10. The bird loves her young no less than Mamma loves us.

11. Let us walk on.

SPELLING.

bound, found, ground, hound, mound, pound, round, sound, wound, abound, aground, around, herself, himself, itself, myself, thyself, yourself.

EXERCISES.

1. The ——— loves her young very much.

2. Does Mamma ——— us more?

3. No, she ——— not.

4. Did ——— take the eggs from the nest?

5. Yes, I ——— them.

6. The mother bird must have been very ——— when she ——— back to her nest.

7. Do you see a bird's nest in the ———?

8. Yes, I _____ there must _____ some eggs in it.
9. Shall I _____ up the tree and take the eggs ?
10. No, you must _____ take them.

WRITING.

Sometime ago when John and I found a birdsnest, we took all the eggs home. The mother bird must have been very sad when she came back to her nest.

LESSON XI.

rāin, rāin'ĭng, härd, rāin'ў(rān'ĭ),
wĕath'ẽr, cẽr'tȧĭnlў(sẽr'tĭnlĭ), cârẹ,
wĕt, stŏp, ȧfrāid', sēȧ'şǫn(sē'zn),
cŏntĭn'ūẹ, thĩr'tў(thẽr'tĭ), hăp'pў(hăp'ĭ),
ō'vẽr.

RAIN.

1. It is raining, isn't it?

2. Yes, it is raining very hard.
3. Shall you go to school in this rainy weather?

4. Certainly! I must go.

5. You must take care not to get wet.

6. Shall you go out if the rain stops?

7. Yes, but I am afraid it will not stop raining very soon.

8. I am getting tired of the rainy season.

9. How long will it continue?

10. Thirty days, I think.

11. How happy we shall be when the rainy season is over!

SPELLING.

cach,	beach,	peach,	reach,	teach,
feat,	heat,	meat,	neat,	seat,
deal,	heal,	meal,	seal,	veal,

weal,   zeal,   season,   reason,   treason,

happy,   poppy,   sappy,   sloppy.

EXERCISES.

1. Is this the rainy _____ ?
2. Yes, but it will soon _____ over.
3. I shall be _____ when it is over.
4. Do you think the rain will _____ very soon ?
5. I am afraid it will _____ stop very soon.
6. Will you _____ out if the rain stops ?
7. Yes, _____ shall.
8. You will get _____ if you go out now.
9. But _____ must go out.
10. It is _____ very hard, isn't it ?

WRITING.

We are getting tired of the rainy season. How long will it continue? Thirty days, I think. How happy we shall be when the rainy season is over! It is raining very hard, isn't it?

LESSON XII.

stănd′ĭng,   bănk,   rĭv′ẽr,   wạ′tẽr,
rŭn′ḥĭng,   răp′ĭdlў(răp′ĭdlĭ),   flōwṣ,
sēạ,   dēẹp,   rāịnẹd,   sŭp̣pōṣẹ′(sŭp̣pōz′),
shăl′lȯw,   drȳ(drī),   brĭdġẹ,
sīdẹ.

THE RIVER.

1. We are now standing on the bank of the river.

2. Look, the water is running quite rapidly.

3. Where does the water come from?

4. It comes from the mountains.

5. Where does it go?

6. It flows into the sea.

7. Is the water always as deep as it is now?

8. O no! We have more water after it has rained.

9. I suppose the water gets shallow when the dry weather continues.

10. You are quite right.

11. Let us walk over the bridge and go to the other side.

12. All right. Come on!

SPELLING.

flow,   hollow,   sallow,   shallow,
wallow,   giver,   liver,   quiver,
river,   shiver,   cunning,   punning,
running,   shunning,   stunning.

EXERCISES.

1. The water _____ not shallow.
2. That is because _____ rained yesterday.
3. I suppose the water gets shallow when the _____ weather continues ?
4. Yes, you are _____ right.
5. Is this a river _____ a sea ?
6. It is not a sea but a _____.
7. Does the water flow _____ the sea ?
8. Yes. How rapidly the water _____ !
9. Where does the _____ come from ?
10. It comes _____ the mountains.

WRITING.

We are now standing on the bank of the river. Look, the water is running very rapidly. Where does it go to? It flows into the sea. Let us walk over the bridge and go to the other side.

43

All right. Come on.

LESSON XIII.

swĭm,   swĭm′mĭng,   lāke,   bāthe,
grĕāt,   fŭn,   thōugh (thō),   fär,
lēast,   quạr′tẽr,   mīle,   jŭmp,
ĕnjoy′ĭng (ĕnjoi′ĭng).

SWIMMING.

1. Let us go down to the lake.
2. Shall we bathe in it?
3. Yes, it will be great fun.
4. Can you swim?
5. Yes, I can, though not very well.
6. How far do you think you can swim?

7. I think I can swim at least a quarter of a mile.

8. Now, jump into the water.

9. You swim much better than I can.

10. How are you enjoying this?
11. I am enjoying it very much.
12. Did you ever swim in the sea?
13. No, never.

SPELLING.

| dough, | though, | bought, | brought, |
| fought, | nought, | ought, | sought, |

thought, wrought, brimming, drumming, grinning, primming, stunning, slipping, smutting, snapping, splitting, stripping, swimming, trimming, whetting.

EXERCISES.

1. He swims very ――――.
2. Can you ―――― better than he does ?
3. I don't think I ――――.
4. How far can ―――― swim ?
5. I can swim a ―――― of a mile.
6. Did you ever swim ―――― the lake ?
7. No, ――――.
8. Will you ―――― into the water ?
9. I can ―――― swim at all.
10. Let us bathe ―――― the water.
11. Isn't this ―――― fun ?
12. I see you ―――― enjoying it.

WRITING.

Let us go down to the lake. Shall we bathe in it? Yes, it will be great fun. How far do you think you can swim? I think I can swim at least a quarter of a mile. Did you ever *swim in the sea? No,*

never.

LESSON XIV.

plāy'ĭng, bāṣe'-ball, băt, pĭtch,
plāyĕd, bĕfôre', cătch, cătch'ẽr,
trȳ(trī), mŏd'ĕst, wĭsh, coụḷd(koŏd)
dĭdn't, chăm'pĭon(chăm'pĭŭn), plāy'ẽr.

PLAYING BALL.

1. Here we are in the playground.
2. Let us play ball.
3. All right. You take the bat and I will pitch.
4. Did you ever play base-ball?
5. Yes, I played a little before I came to this school.

6. Who will be the catcher?
7. I will try though I am not a good one.
8. You are very modest, but you catch very well.

9. I wish I could catch as well as you can.
10. Didn't you know he is the champion player of the school?
11. No, I didn't.

SPELLING.

butcher,   catcher,   pitcher,   stitcher,
stretcher,   thatcher,   badge,   budge,
dodge,   hedge,   judge,   ridge,
bridge,   drudge,   grudge,   pledge,
sledge.

EXERCISES.

1. Do you know he——the champion player ?
2. O yes, he is a very good ——— .
3. Can you pitch the ball as ——— as he can ?
4. I wish I ——— .
5. You are a ——— catcher.
6. When did ——— play ball ?
7. Before I ——— to this school.
8. Who will ——— the catcher ?
9. I think I will ———.
10. Let us all ——— ball in this playground.

WRITING.

Who will be the catcher?
I will try though I am
not a good one. You are
very modest, but you catch
quite well. I wish I could
pitch as well as you can.

Didn't you know he is

the champion player of the school?

LESSON XV.

bōwl, grāçe'fullȳ(grās'fŏŏlĭ), swĭmṣ,
caught(kạt), hŏŏk, līnẹ,
won'dẽr(wŭn'der) līvẹ, dīe.

FISH.

1. Look at the fish in the bowl.

2. How gracefully it swims in the water!

3. Did you catch it yourself?

4. No. My uncle caught it in the river and gave it to me.

5. Do you know how it was caught?

6. I suppose it was caught with hook and line.

7. I wonder if it is as happy in the bowl as in the river.

8. O no! It can't be.

9. Then, it will not live long in this bowl.

10. I am afraid it will soon die, if I do not take very good care of it.

SPELLING.

compose,   depose,   dispose,   propose,
repose,   suppose,   under,   sunder,
blunder,   plunder,   wonder,   ant,
can't,   pant,   grant,   slant,
plant.

EXERCISES.

1. Will the _____ live long in the bowl ?
2. It may _____ if I do not take very good care of it.
3. The fish does _____ seem to be happy.
4. It can't _____ happy in the bowl.
5. My uncle caught it _____ hook and line.
6. Where did he _____ it ?
7. He caught it in the _____.
8. How gracefully the fish _____ !
9. Who gave the fish _____ you ?
10. My _____ gave it to me.

WRITING.

I wonder if the fish is as happy in the bowl as in the river. O no! It can't be. Then, it will not live long in the bowl. I am afraid it will soon die, if I do not take very good care of it.

LESSON XVI.

lămp, rēạd′ĭng, w̌rīt′ĭng, dŏẹṣn't(dŭznt), līg̑ht(līt), ĭndēẹd′(ĭndēd′), oil, a′ny(ĕ′nĭ), găs, ĕlĕc′trĭc(ĕlĕk′trĭk), sēẹn, ē′vẹnĭng.

THE LAMP.

1. What is that on the table?
2. It is a lamp.
3. What are John and Mary doing there?
4. John is reading and Mary is writing.

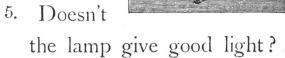

5. Doesn't the lamp give good light?
6. Yes, it does indeed.

7. Is it an oil lamp?

8. Yes, it is an oil lamp.

9. Are there any other kinds of lamps?

10. There are gas lamps and electric lamps.

11. I don't think I have ever seen them.

12. If you come to my house some evening, I will show them to you.

SPELLING.

might,	horse,	strong,	young,
should,	does,	bathe,	nickel,
raining,	played,	don't,	writing.

EXERCISES.

1. Do you see the lamp —— the table ?
2. Yes, I —— it very well.
3. Doesn't the lamp give good —— ?
4. Yes, it —— .
5. Do you think it —— an oil —— ?
6. I do not —— it is an oil lamp.
7. Is it —— electric lamp ?
8. No, it is —— an electric lamp, —— a gas lamp.
9. I have —— seen a gas lamp before.
10. What are the boy —— the girl doing there ?
11. The boy —— reading and —— girl is writing.
12. If you come to my house some ——, I will —— you electric lamps.

WRITING.

Doesn't the lamp give good light? Yes, it does indeed. There are many kinds of lamps. Oil lamps, gas lamps, and electric lamps. If you come to my house some *evening, I will show you electric lamps.*

LESSON XVII.

flăg, Jăpȧnesė'(jăpŭnēz'),
sĕc'ȯnd(sĕk'ŭnd), Eng'land(ĭng'lŭnd),
thîrd(thẽrd), Ȧmĕr'ĭcȧ(ȧmĕr'ĭkȧ),
Ȧmĕr'ĭcan(ȧmĕr'ĭkŭn), fouȓth,
Ġẽr'man(jẽr'mŭn), Ġẽr'manў(jẽr'mŭnĭ),
fĭfth, Frȧnçė(frȧns), Frĕnch,
Rŭs'ṣian(rŭsh'ŭn), Chī'nȧ, Chīnēsė'.

FLAGS.

1. What are all these?
2. These are flags.
3. The first one is the Japanese flag.
4. The second one is the

flag of England.

5. Yes, it is the English flag.

6. Do you know the third one?

7. I think it is the flag of America.

8. Yes, it is the American flag.

9. And the fourth?

10. It is the German flag— the flag of Germany.

11. Isn't the fifth one the flag of France?

12. Yes, it is the French flag.

13. Is the last one the Russian flag?

14. No. It is the Chinese flag.

SPELLING.

after, brighter, clever, didn't,
school, follow, garden, modest,
third, summer, shallow, caught.

EXERCISES.

1. Which _____ the Japanese flag?
2. The first _____ is the Japanese flag.
3. Do you know _____ second flag?
4. Yes, it is the _____ flag.
5. Have _____ ever seen the third flag?
6. O yes! That is the American _____.
7. What _____ the next?
8. The next must _____ the German flag.
9. And _____ fifth?
10. The fifth is the _____ flag.
11. The _____ is the Chinese flag.

WRITING.

Japan, England, America, Germany, France, China. These are six flags. I know them all. The first one is the Japanese flag. The second one is the flag

of England. Yes, it is
the English flag. The
third is the American
flag. The fourth is the
German flag. Do you
know the fifth? Yes, it
is the French flag. The

last is the Chinese flag.

LESSON XVIII.

pōst-ŏf'fĭçĕ(pōst-ŏf'ĭs), tĭlļ, gŏŏd-bȳ̆',
càn't(kànt), fâst'ĕr, bĕst.

PAPA AND MAMMA.

1. Papa, where are you going?
2. I am going to the post-office.
3. May I go with you?
4. Yes, Henry, you may.
5. Will you take Mary with you also?
6. I am afraid she cannot walk so far.

7. Mamma, you and I will stay home till Papa and Henry come back from the post-office.

8. Yes, you are a very good girl.
9. Good-bye, Mary. We shall be back very soon.
10. Good-bye, Henry.
11. Come on, Henry. Can't you walk any faster?

12. No, Papa. This is the best I can do.

SPELLING.

water,	thirty,	standing,	reading,
playing,	can't,	Japan,	England,
ago,	rainy,	honey,	enjoying.

EXERCISES.

1. Is Papa going to the ——— ?
2. Yes, Papa is ——— to the post-office.
3. Will he take Henry ——— him ?
4. Yes, but he will ——— take Mary with him.
5. Do you think Mary can ——— so far ?
6. No, I do not ——— so.
7. Mamma and Mary will stay ——— .
8. Papa and Henry will ——— back very soon.
9. Can't Henry walk ——— faster ?
10. No; that is the best he ——— do.

WRITING.

I am going to the post-office. May I go with you? Yes, Henry, you may. Will you take Mary with you also? I am afraid she can not walk so far. Mamma and

68

I will stay home till Papa and Henry come back

LESSON XIX.

răts, flŏçk, flŏçk'ĭng, cŭp'board(kŭb'bẽrd), sŏme'thĭng(sŭm'thĭng), därk, dāy'līght, trăp, slȳ(slī), ŏf'tẹn(ŏf'n), bȳ, mewẹd(mūd), wou̯ld(wŏŏd), awāy', scârẹd, kĭll.

THE RATS.

1. Look at the rats flocking to the cupboard.

2. What do they flock to the cupboard for ?

3. They are looking for something to eat.

4. Can they see in the dark?
5. Yes, they can see in the dark as well as in daylight.

6. Can you catch them with a trap?
7. Yes, but they are very sly.
8. Though they are sly, they are often caught by the cat, aren't they?
9. If a cat mewed here, all these rats would run away.
10. Why would they be so scared?
11. Because the cat would catch and kill them.

70

SPELLING.

aren't,   beehive,   father,   away,
any,   French,   German,   American,
English,   Japanese,   pretty,   sometimes.

EXERCISES.

1. The rats are ———— to the cupboard.
2. What are ——— looking for ?
3. They are looking for ——— to eat.
4. Can they ——— when it is dark ?
5. O yes, they can see in the ——— very well.
6. Did you ever catch a rat with a ——— ?
7. Yes, I caught one ——— a trap.
8. Aren't they ——— sly ?
9. Yes, but they are often ——— by the cat.
10. Would they ——— away if a cat mewed here ?
11. Certainly, for the cat would catch and ——— them.

WRITING.

What do the rats flock
to the cupboard for?
They are looking for
something to eat. Though
they are very sly, they
are often caught by the
cat, aren't they? If a

cat mewed here, all these rats would run away. Why would they be so scared? Because the cat would catch and kill them.

LESSON XX.

tạḷḷ,   mōst,   cȯv′ẽrẹd(cŭv′ẽrd),
lēȧvẹṣ(lèvz), grēẹn(grēn), yĕl′ḷȯẇ(yĕl′ȯ̇),
sĭng,   wĭnd,   blōẇṣ(blōz),   fạḷḷ,
rē̆māịn′,   cạḷḷ,   sŭch,   ĕv′ẽr-grēẹn.

THE WOOD.

1. We are now in the wood.
2. Aren't the trees all very tall?
3. Most of the trees are covered with leaves.

4. Some of the leaves are green, and others are yellow.
5. Do you hear some birds singing in the trees?
6. Yes, I do. What can those birds be?
7. When the wind blows the leaves will fall.
8. Will all the leaves fall?
9. No, most of those green leaves will remain on the trees.
10. What do you call such trees?
11. We call them ever-green trees.

SPELLING.

scared,	rapidly,	player,	mewed,
highest,	fifty,	together,	catcher,
pitcher,	leaves,	minute.	

EXERCISES.

1. The trees in the ——— are very tall.
2. Are they covered ——— leaves ?
3. Yes, most ——— the trees are covered with leaves.
4. Do you ——— some birds singing in the trees ?
5. Yes, I do, but I do not know ——— they are.
6. Will the leaves ——— when the wind blows ?
7. Some will fall, ——— the others will not.
8. The green leaves ——— not fall.
9. The yellow ——— will fall.
10. What are ever-green ——— ?
11. They are the trees always ——— with green leaves.

WRITING.

Most of the trees are covered with leaves. When the wind blows, the leaves will fall. Will all the leaves fall? Though the yellow leaves may fall, most of the green leaves

will remain on the trees.
What do you call such
trees? We call them ever-
green trees.

LESSON XXI.

fīrẹ,　bā′sịn,　drạẉn,　wĕlḷ,
nẹī′thẽr(nī′thĕr),　nôr(nạr),　rĭv′ẽr-wạ′tẽr,
rāịn′-wạ′tẽr,　prĕ̄fẽr′,　drĭnk,
sprĭng′-wạ′tẽr,　pūrẹ,　stōvẹ,
boil′ĭng,　wạrm,　ourselvẹ̱s′,
ḝssĕn′tial(ĕ-sĕn′-shŭl),　līfẹ.

WATER AND FIRE.

1. The basin is full of water.
2. Where did the water come from?
3. This water was drawn from the well.
4. It is neither river-water, nor rain-water.
5. I prefer to drink spring-water.
6. Is spring-water always pure and good to drink?
7. Not always.
8. Fire is in the stove.
9. Water is boiling on the stove.
10. We warm ourselves before the stove.

11. Water and fire are quite essential to our life.

12. Were there no water or fire, we should all die.

SPELLING.

boiling, collect, continue, drawn, good-bye, hundred, ourselves, post-office, second, something, often.

EXERCISES.

1. Do you see water in the ——— ?
2. Yes, the basin is ——— of water.

3. Was the water —— from the well ?
4. No; it is either river-water——rain-water.
5. Which water is best to —— ?
6. I —— not know.
7. What is boiling —— the stove ?
8. We warm —— before the stove.
9. Water and fire are —— to our life.
10. If there —— no water or fire, we should<
    all —— .

WRITING.

This water was drawn from the well. I prefer to drink spring-water.

Water is boiling over the stove. We warm ourselves before the fire.   Water and fire are quite essential to our life.   Were there no water or fire, we should all die.

LESSON XXII.

cär′riàġe(kăr′ĭj), whom(hōōm) their(thâr),
draw′ing, stout, tāk′ĕn,
rĭd′dĕn, jĭnrĭkĭshă, ĕxpĕn′sĭve,
pē′ople(pē′pl), hăd, săt′ĭsfĭed.

THE CARRIAGE.

1. Whom do you see in the carriage?

2. I see Frank, and Lucy, and their father.
3. How many horses are drawing the carriage?
4. Two stout horses are drawing it.
5. Have you ever taken a ride in a carriage?
6. No; but I have often ridden in a jinrikisha.
7. A carriage is more expensive than a jinrikisha, isn't it?
8. O yes. Very few people can have a carriage.
9. I wish I had one.
10. Do you? As for me, I am quite satisfied with what I have.

SPELLING.

yellow,   taken,   spring-water,   remain,
prefer,   mother,   faster,   whom,
drawing,   their,   covered,   basin.

EXERCISES.

1. Frank and Lucy are ＿＿＿ the carriage.
2. I see their ＿＿＿ also.
3. Two stout ＿＿＿ are drawing the carriage.
4. Have you ever ＿＿＿ in a carriage?
5. No; I have ＿＿＿ taken a ride in a carriage.
6. Which is the more expensive, a carriage ＿＿＿ a jinrikisha?
7. A carriage is more ＿＿＿ than a jinrikisha.
8. Then, many ＿＿＿ can not have a carriage.
9. I wish I ＿＿＿ a carriage.
10. As for me, I am quite ＿＿＿ with what I have.

WRITING.

A carriage is more expensive than a jinrikisha, isn't it? O yes, very few people can have a carriage. I wish I had a carriage. Do you? As for me, I am quite satisfied with what I have.

LESSON XXIII.

fruit(froot), ŏr'ăngĕs̱, peạch'ĕs̱, pẹârs̱,
waịt,   grō'çẽr's̱(grō'sẽr'z),   häḷf,
pā'tient(pā'shĕnt),   hĕlp,   I'lḷ(īl).

FRUIT.

1. Are you fond of fruit?
2. Yes, I am fond of all kinds of fruit.
3. Here we have some apples and oranges.

4. I wish we had some peaches and pears.

5. Do you like peaches and pears better than apples and oranges?

6. No, but my mother does.

7. But you know it is not the season for peaches and pears.

8. How long shall we have to wait before we find them at the grocer's?

9. We must wait for at least half a year.

10. So long as that?

11. Yes, we must be patient.

12. Help yourself to an apple or an orange.

13. I'll thank you for an apple.

SPELLING.

carriage,	expensive,	people,	peaches,
fruit,	busy,	weather,	daytime,
certainly,	France,	fourth,	because,
least,	always,	sunrise,	ridden.

EXERCISES.

1. Which fruit _____ you like best?
2. I _____ apples best.
3. I wish you _____ some peaches.
4. Are you fond _____ peaches?
5. My mother is _____ of peaches and pears.
6. It is not the season _____ them.
7. When shall we _____ peaches and pears at the grocer's?
8. You will have to wait for half a _____.
9. Help _____ to an orange.
10. Thank you _____ much.

WRITING.

Do you like peaches and pears better than apples and oranges? No, but my mother does. But you know it is not the season for them. How long shall we have to wait before we

90

find them at the grocer's?

At least half a year.

So long as that? Yes, we

must be patient.

LESSON XXIV.

cows(kouz), mĕȧd′ȯw(mĕd′ō),
färm′ẽr, mĭlk′ĭng, wīfẹ,
căr′rўĭng(kăr′-ĭ-ĭng), mĭlk,
ĕmploy′ẹd(ĕmploid′), fĭẹld, ŏx,
pûr′pose(pûr′pŭs), flĕsh, dēȧl, bēẹf.

COWS.

1. Look at the cows in the meadow.

2. They are all very big and fat, aren't they?
3. The farmer is milking the cows, and his wife is carrying the milk to the house.

4. All these cows do not give milk, do they?
5. No, some of them are employed in the fields.
6. An ox is better for that purpose than a cow.

7. Do you eat the flesh of a cow or an ox?

8. O yes, we eat a great deal of it.

9. What do you call it?

10. It is called beef.

SPELLING.

afraid,   carrying,   employed,   farmer,
grocer's,   lily,   meadow,   milking,
patient,   purpose,   America.

EXERCISES.

1. I see many cows in the _____ .

2. These cows are all very _____ and _____ .

3. The farmer is milking the _____ .

4. His wife is _____ the milk to the house.

5. Do all these cows _____ milk?

6. No; some of them are _____ in the fields.

7. Isn't an ox better _____ the purpose?

8. Do you eat the _____ of a cow or an ox ?
9. Yes, I eat a great _____ of it.
10. It is called _____ .

WRITING.

Look at the cows in the
meadow. They are all
very big and fat, aren't
they? The farmer is milk-
ing the cows, and his wife

is carrying the milk to
the house. Some of the
cows are employed in the
fields. Do you eat beef?
Yes, we eat a great deal
of it.

95

LESSON XXV.

snōw, snōw'měn, māk'ĭng,
snōw'man(snō'mŭn), cârȩ'fullў(kâr'foŏlĭ),
donȩ(dŭn), hĕlpȩd(hĕlpt), tāstȩ,
hẽrs, poōr, shôrt, mĕlt, lŏng'ẽr,
theirs(thârz), ꞓᴉ̄rȩ'lў(shoōr'lĭ), shôrt'ẽr.
ours.

SNOW.

1. Snow! Snow!

2. Indeed! How beautiful it is!

3. Let us all go out and make snowmen.

4. John is making a **very large** snowman.

5. George's snowman is not so large, but quite carefully made.

6. Is this yours or his?

7. It is mine. How do you like it?

8. It is fine—very well done!
9. Kate helped me make it.
10. Our taste is not so good as hers.

11. Poor snowmen! Their life is very short, for they will melt away when the sun shines on them.
12. Well, but our life may not be much longer than theirs.
13. Surely their life is far shorter than ours.

SPELLING.

essential,　cupboard,　quarter,　snowman,

gracefully,　pears,　other,　making,

longer,　done,　indeed,　I'll.

EXERCISES.

1. Snow is indeed —— .
2. We shall go out and —— snowmen.
3. John's snowman is —— large.
4. George has made his snowman quite——.
5. Is this yours —— hers ?
6. It is very well ——.
7. She helped me —— the snowman.
8. How good her taste —— !
9. Poor snowmen ! They will —— away when the sun —— on them.
10. Their life is much —— than ours.

WRITING.

John is making a very large snowman. George's snowman is not so large, but quite carefully made. Poor snowmen! Their life is very short, for they will melt away when the

sun shines on them. Well,
but our life may not be
much longer than theirs.
Surely their life is far
shorter than ours.

LESSON XXVI.

món'keys(mŭn'kĭz),   sĕv'ēral(sĕv'ērŭl),

mónths(mŭnths),   páss'ĭng,   throȗgh(thrōō),

walk'ĭng,   ground,   hīgh(hī),

pecul'iar(pĕkūl'yēr),   noise(noiz),

ĕnjoyed'(ĕnjoid'),   coȗldn't(kŏŏdnt),

quĭck'lў(quĭk'lĭ),   ēas'ĭlў(ēz'ĭlĭ),   **shŏt,**

ĕntrăpped'(ĕntrăpt').

MONKEYS.

1. Have you ever seen a monkey?
2. Yes, I have seen several monkeys.
3. When did you see them?
4. I saw them a few months ago, when my father and I were passing through the mountains.
5. Were they walking on the ground?

6. They were high up in the trees and making a peculiar noise.

7. I wish I had been there with you.

8. So do I. You would have enjoyed it.

9. Couldn't you catch them?

10. O no! They climb up the trees so quickly, and jump from tree to tree so easily.

11. But they do often get caught, don't they?

12. Yes, when they are shot or entrapped.

SPELLING.

couldn't,	enjoyed,	easily,	entrapped,
helped,	monkey,	passing,	noise,
quickly,	surely,	shorter,	through.

EXERCISES.

1. I ＿＿ seen several monkeys.
2. When did you ＿＿ them ?
3. I saw them a ＿＿ months ago.
4. Were they walking ＿＿ the ground ?
5. O no, they were up in the＿＿and making a ＿＿ noise.
6. I wish I ＿＿ seen them.
7. So do I.　You would ＿＿ enjoyed it.
8. They climb up the trees so ＿＿, and jump from tree to tree so ＿＿.
9. But they do often ＿＿ caught, don't they ?
10. Yes, when they ＿＿ shot or entrapped.

WRITING.

When did you see monkeys?
I saw them a few months
ago, when my father and
I were passing through the
mountains. They were high
up in the trees, and making
a peculiar noise. Couldn't
you catch them? O no.

They climb up the trees so quickly, and jump from tree to tree so easily.

LESSON XXVII.

āgᵉ, yēᵃrs, Tanaka, foᵤr′tēᵉn(fōr′tēn), yĕs′tērdāy, ōld′ĕst, clᴀss(klᴀs), Sugi, stū′dĕnt, yọŭng′ĕst(yŭng′ĕst), rōōm, Kodama, smᴀll′ĕst, Harada, Nakano.

AGE.

1. How old are you?
2. I am thirteen years old.

3. Is Mr. Tanaka older than you?

4. Yes, he was fourteen yesterday.

5. Who is the oldest boy in the class?

6. Mr. Sugi is the oldest, and the best student too.

7. Who is the youngest boy in the room?

8. Mr. Kodama is the youngest, but **not** the smallest.

9. Mr. Harada **is very tall for his age,** isn't he?

10. Mr. Nakano is very clever for his age.

11. You are all very young, much younger than I.

SPELLING.

different, fourteen, months, oldest,
evening, several, student, smallest,
youngest.

EXERCISES.

1. Mr. Tanaka, how old ＿＿ you?
2. I ＿＿ fourteen yesterday.
3. Is Mr. Kodama younger ＿＿ you?
4. Yes, sir. He is a year ＿＿ than I.
5. Who is the oldest boy in the ＿＿?
6. Mr. Harada is the ＿＿, and the best student too.
7. Who ＿＿ the youngest boy in the room?
8. I am the youngest but not the ＿＿.
9. You are all ＿＿ than I.

WRITING.

Mr. Sugi is the oldest boy in the class, and the best student too. Mr. Kodama is the youngest boy in the room, but not the smallest. Mr. Nakano is very clever for his age. Mr. Harada is *very tall for his age, isn't he?*

LESSON XXVIII.

sāil′bōat(sāl′bōt), stēam′bōat(stēm′bōt), trăv′ĕl, dĭs′tançe(dĭs′tŭns), wạr′shĭp, pĭc′tūres(pĭk′tūrz), wạr′shĭps, rē′al(rē′ŭl), rōw, ôught(at).

THE SAILBOAT AND THE STEAMBOAT.

1. Can you tell me what this is?

2. Yes, sir. That is a sailboat.

3. Can a sailboat travel as fast as a steamboat?

4. No, it cannot.
5. This is a steamboat, isn't it?
6. Yes, it is.
7. Did you ever travel in a steamboat?
8. Yes, but only for a short distance.

9. Have you ever seen a warship?
10. I have seen many pictures of warships, but no real one.
11. Can you row?
12. No, I can't.
13. You ought to learn.

SPELLING.

electric,   ever-green,   distance,   satisfied,
peculiar,   ought,   pictures,   real,
sailboat,   steamboat,   warship,   travel.

EXERCISES.

1. Is ——— a sailboat ?

2. No, it ——— a steamboat.

3. Does a steamboat ——— faster than a sailboat ?

4. O yes, very much ———.

5. Have you ever ——— in a steamboat ?

6. Yes, but for a short ———.

7. Have you ever ——— a warship ?

8. I have seen many ——— of warships.

9. Can ——— row ?

10. No. I ought ——— learn.

WRITING.

Can a sailboat run as fast as a steamboat? No, it cannot. Did you ever travel in a steamboat?

Yes, but only for a short distance. Have you ever seen a warship? I have seen many pictures of war

ships, but no real one. If

you do not know how to

row, you ought to learn.

LESSON XXIX.

cŏl′ourṣ(kŭl′ẽrz),　stĭlļ,　brīg̣ht′ĕst(brīt′ĕst),
cleạr,　　　skȳ(skī),　　blu̱e̱,　　　pûr′ple̱,
vī′ōlĕt,　grȧsṣ.

COLOURS.

1. Some of these roses are red, others
   are white, and still others are yellow.
2. Which is the brightest of these
   three colours?

3. Red is by far the brightest.
4. What colour do red and yellow make?

5. Red and yellow make orange.
6. What is the colour of the clear sky?
7. It is blue.
8. What colours do blue and red make?
9. Blue and red make purple and violet.

10. What colour do blue and yellow make?

11. Blue and yellow make green—the colour of grass.

12. What other colour do you know?

13. I know black.

SPELLING.

brightest,   colours,   purple,   violets,
snowmen,   walking,   younger,   mountain,
yesterday,   champion,   horseback,   fifteen.

EXERCISES.

1. Is red a bright ——— ?
2. Yes, it is a very ——— colour.
3. What do blue and red ——— ?
4. Blue and red make ——— and ———.
5. What ——— the colour of the clear sky?

6. It is ——— .
7. What do red ——— yellow make?
8. Red and ——— make orange.
9. Green is the colour of ——— .
10. Violet is the ——— of the violet.

WRITING.

Some of these roses are red, others are white, and still others are yellow. Which is the brightest of these three colours? Red is by

far the brightest.   Red
and yellow make orange.
Blue and red make pur-
ple and violet.
Blue and yellow make
green—the colour of grass.
The blue sky and the green
grass.

LESSON XXX.

ĕnd, Lĭz'z̧ĭē(lĭz'ĭ), mēa̧n, a̓gain'(a̓gĕn'), grăd'ūatĕd(grăd'ūatĕd), hīgh'ẽr(hī'ẽr), bŏd'ȳ(bŏd'ĭ), sŏr'ɾȳ(sŏr'ĭ), pärt, frḭĕnds̰(frĕndz), hōpe̥, fŏrgĕt'.

THE END OF THE SCHOOL YEAR.

1. Frank and Lizzie are brother and sister.
2. Aren't they going out of the school?
3. Yes, they are — not to come back again.

4. What do you mean?
5. They have been graduated from the school.
6. How happy they must be!
7. Will they go to a higher school?
8. They may, but nobody knows.
9. They must be sorry to part from their teachers and friends.
10. I hope they will not forget what they have learned in this school.

SPELLING.

Germany, blue, carefully, forget,
higher, Lizzie, George, Henry,
nobody, sorry, theirs.

EXERCISES.

1. Frank and Lizzie are brother and ———.
2. They are going out ——— the school.
3. They are not to come back here ———.

4. Have they been graduated ——— the school?
5. Yes, how happy ——— must be!
6. Will they go to a ——— school?
7. They may, but nobody ———.
8. They must be sorry to ——— from their friends.
9. I hope they will not forget ——— they have learned here.

WRITING.

Frank and Lizzie are

going out of the school—

not to come back again.

They have been graduated

from the school. They may
go to a higher school.

They must be sorry to
part from their teachers
and friends. I hope they
will not forget what they
have learned in this school.

WORD LIST

a,	about,	afraid,	after,
again,	age,	ago,	all,
alphabet,	also,	always,	am,
America,	American,	an,	and,
any,	apples,	are,	aren't,
as,	at,	aunt,	away,
back,	bad,	ball,	bank,
base-ball,	basin,	basket,	bat,
bathe,	be,	beautiful,	because,
beef,	beehive,	been,	bees,
before(adv.),	before(conj.),	believe,	bench,
best,	better,	big,	bird,
bird's,	birds,	black,	blows,
blue,	body,	boiling,	both,
bowl,	box,	boy,	boys,
brick,	bridge,	bright,	brighter,
brightest,	brother,	busy,	but,
by,	call,	called,	came,
can,	cannot,	can't,	cap,
capital,	care,	carefully,	carriage,

carrying,	cat,	catch,	catcher,
caught,	certainly,	chair,	champion,
Charles,	China,	Chinese,	class,
clear,	clever,	climb,	close(adj.),
coin,	collect,	colour,	come,
continue,	copper,	could,	couldn't,
count,	covered,	cows,	cupboard,
dark,	daylight,	days,	daytime,
deal,	deep,	desk,	did,
didn't,	die,	different,	distance,
do,	does,	doesn't,	dog,
doing,	doll,	done,	don't,
door,	down,	drawing,	drawn,
drink,	dry,	each,	ear,
easily,	eat,	eggs,	eight,
electric,	eleven,	employed,	end,
England,	English,	enjoyed,	enjoying,
enough,	entrapped,	essential,	evening,
ever,	ever-green,	expensive,	eye,
face,	fall,	far,	farmer,
fast,	faster,	fat,	father,

feed,	feeds,	feet,	few,
field,	fifteen,	fifth,	fifty,
find,	fine,	finger,	finish,
fire,	first,	fish,	five,
flag,	flags,	flesh,	flock,
flocking,	floor,	flower,	flowers,
flows,	follows,	fond,	foot,
for(prep.),	for(conj.),	forget,	found,
four,	fourteen,	fourth,	France,
Frank,	Frank's,	French,	friends,
from,	fruit,	Fuji,	full,
fun,	garden,	gas,	gave,
George's,	German,	Germany,	get,
getting,	girl,	girls,	give,
go,	goes,	going,	gold,
good,	good-bye,	gracefully,	graduated,
grand,	grass,	great,	green,
grocer's,	ground,	gun,	had,
half,	Hana,	hand,	happy,
Harada,	hard,	has,	hat,
have,	he,	hear,	help,

helped,	Henry,	her,	here,
hers,	herself,	high,	higher,
highest,	hills,	him,	his,
home,	honey,	hook,	hope,
horse,	horses,	horse-back,	house,
how,	hundred,	I,	if,
I'll,	in,	indeed,	ink,
inkstand,	into,	is,	isn't,
it,	Japan,	Japanese,	jinrikisha,
Jiro,	John,	jump,	just,
Kate,	keep,	kill,	kind(adj.),
kinds,	Kinzo,	kitten,	know,
knows,	Kodama,	lake,	lamp,
lamps,	lap,	large,	larger,
last,	learn,	learned,	least,
leaves,	left(adj.),	left(past),	less,
let,	letter,	life,	light,
like(adj.),	like(verb),	likes,	lilies,
line,	little,	live,	Lizzie,
long,	longer,	look,	looked,
looking,	loves,	Lucy,	made,

make,	making,	Mamma,	man,
many,	Mary,	may,	me,
meadow,	mean,	melt,	mewed,
might,	mile,	milk,	milking,
mine,	minutes,	modest,	monkey,
monkeys,	morning,	month,	months,
moon,	more,	most,	mother,
mount,	mountain,	mountains,	mouth,
Mr.,	Mrs.,	much	must,
my,	nail,	Nakano,	name,
neither,	nest,	never,	new,
next,	nickel,	night,	Niitakayama,
nine,	Nishimura,	no,	nobody,
noise,	nor,	nose,	not,
now,	O,	oblige,	of,
often,	oh,	oil,	old,
older,	oldest,	on,	one,
only,	open,	or,	orange,
other,	others,	ought,	our,
ours,	ourselves,	out,	over,
ox,	Papa,	paper,	part,

passing,	patient,	peaches,	pears,
peculiar,	pen,	pencil,	penknife,
people,	pick,	pictures,	pitch,
play,	please,	pocket,	poor,
played,	player,	playground,	playing,
post-office,	prefer,	pretty,	proud,
pure,	purple,	purpose,	put,
quarter,	quickly,	quite,	rain,
rained,	raining,	rain-water,	rainy,
rapidly,	rats,	reached,	read,
reader,	reading,	real,	red,
remain,	rice,	ridden,	ride(noun),
ride(verb),	right,	*rin*,	rise,
river,	river-water,	room,	roses,
round,	row,	Roy,	run,
running,	Russian,	sad,	sailboat,
satisfied,	saw,	say,	scared,
school,	sea,	season,	seat,
second,	see,	seems,	seen,
sen,	seven,	several,	shall,
shallow,	she,	shine,	shines,

shoes, short, shorter, shot,

should, show, shut, side,

silver, sing, sir, sister,

sit, six, sky, sly,

small, smallest, snow, snowman,

snowmen, so, some, something,

sometime, sometimes, soon, sorry,

speak, Spot, spring-water, square,

stand, standing, stars, stay,

steamboat, still, sting, stop,

stops, stout, stove, strong,

student, such, Sugi, summer,

sun, sunrise, suppose, surely,

sweet, swim, swimming, swims,

table, take, taken, tall,

Tanaka, Taro, taste, teacher,

teachers, tell, ten, Terry,

than, thank, that, the,

their, theirs, them, then,

there, these, they, thick,

thin, things, think, third,

thirteen,	thirty,	this,	those,
though,	three,	through,	till,
tired,	to,	toe,	together,
too,	took,	top,	trap,
travel,	tree,	trees,	try,
twelve,	twenty,	two,	Ume,
uncle,	under,	up,	us,
very,	violet,	wait,	walk,
walking,	want,	warm,	warship,
warships,	was,	watch,	water,
way,	we,	weather,	week,
well(noun),	well(adv.),	were,	wet,
what,	when,	where,	which,
while,	white,	who,	whom,
whose,	why,	wife,	will,
wind,	wish,	with,	wonder,
wood,	work,	would,	wright,
writing,	year,	years,	yellow,
yen,	yes,	yesterday,	you,
young,	younger,	youngest,	your,
yours,	yourself.		

明治四十二年 三 月廿七日印　　刷
明治四十二年 三 月三十日發　　行
大正十一年 一 月二十二日修正再版印刷
大正十一年 一 月二十五日修正再版發行

リーダー卷貳定價金拾四錢
大正十一年度臨時定價金拾八錢

著作權者　　文　部　省
發　行　者　株式會社　國定敎科書共同販賣所
　　　　　　東京市日本橋區新右衞門町十六番地

　　代表者　　大　橋　新　太　郞
印　刷　者　　伊　藤　貴　志
　　　　　凸版印刷株式會社代表者
　　　　　東京市下谷區二長町一番地
印　刷　所　　凸版印刷株式會社
　　　　　東京市下谷區二長町一番地

發行所　株式會社　國定敎科書共同販賣所
　　　　東京市日本橋區新右衞門町十六番地

大正十二年度臨時定價金拾六錢

THE MOMBUSHŌ ENGLISH READERS

FOR

ELEMENTARY SCHOOLS

No. 3

THE
MOMBUSHO
ENGLISH READERS

FOR

ELEMENTARY SCHOOLS

NO. 3

KOKUTEIKYŌKASHO KYŌDŌHANBAISHO

TŌKYŌ AND ŌSAKA

LESSON I.

hăllō′, now-a-days(nou′-à-dās), nīçe̱′lў,
Jĕn′nḭē, hĕa̱lth, used(yoost), tro̱ŭ′ble̱,
stŏm′ăcḫ, pärk, pâr′ĕnts, ĕxpĕct′,
ō′clŏc̱k′, rēmĕm′bẽr, kīnd′lў.

THE FRIENDS.

1. Good mornig, Charles.
2. Hallo, Henry! Good morning.

3. How are you getting on now-a-days?
4. Very nicely, thank you.

5. How do you do, Jennie?
6. I am quite well, thank you.
7. Is your brother in good health?
8. No, he is not so well as he used to be.
9. What is the trouble?
10. He seems to have some trouble with his stomach.
11. Come, let us take a walk in the park.
12. I wish I could go with you.
13. Why can't you?
14. My parents expect me at 10 o'clock.
15. Good-bye, then.
16. Please remember me kindly to your parents.
17. I will, thank you.

LESSON II.

chĭld′rĕn, sāmè, lōw̧′ẽr, căr′rў,
pĕn′ḵnīvès, etc.(ĕt-çaèt′ẽra), rēad′ĭng,
w̧rīt′ĭng, arĭth′mētĭc, favorite(fa′vẽrĭt),
stŭd′ў, hĭs′tōrў, geography(jĕog′rafĭ).

THE SCHOOL-CHILDREN.

1. These are school-children.
2. Some of them are boys, and the others are girls.

3. The boys and the girls go to the same school.

4. Do you think they are all in the same class?

5. O no! The big ones are in the higher class, and the little ones are in the lower class.

6. What do they carry in their bags?

7. They carry books, paper, pencils, penknives, etc.

8. I suppose some children like to play in the fields more than to go to school.

9. Yes, I am sorry to say that there are many such.

10, Which do you like better, reading or writing?

11. I like writing better.

12. How do you like arithmetic?

13. Arithmetic is my favorite study.

14. I am also very fond of history and geography.

LESSON III.

traın, rĕạd'y̆, station(stā'shŭn), engine (ĕn'jĭn), smōkẹ, coming(kŭm'ĭng), ĭts, fŭn'nĕl, păs'sĕnġẽrs, hăvẹn't, gŏt, tĭçk'ĕt, yĕt, Ōsȧkȧ, chĕçk, baggage(băg'ĭj), stärt, cär, full(fo͝ol), we're(wēr), ŏff.

THE TRAIN.

1. The train is ready to leave the station.

2. Look at the big engine and the smoke coming out of its funnel.

3. Many passengers are running to catch the train.

4. Are you going to take this train?

5. Yes, but I haven't got my ticket yet.

6. How far do you go?

7. I go as far as Ōsaka.

8. Here is your ticket; you must check your baggage.

9. The train will start in a minute.

10. We must say good-bye to our friends.

11. Let us get in this car, for the others are all full.

12. Take your seat on this side.

13. Now we're off!

LESSON IV.

zoological(zō̆ŏlŏj′ĭkŭl), wĕnt, wīld, animals(ăn′ĭmŭls), lions(lī′ŭns), tī′gẽrs, bẹ̄ârs, Ĭn′dĭȧ, Ăf′rĭcȧ, Hokkaidō, ĭn′tĕrĕsting, elephant(ĕl′ėfŭnt), ĕlsẹ, căm′ĕls, snākẹs, crānẹs.

THE ZOOLOGICAL GARDEN.

1. Have you been to the zoological garden at Ueno?

2. Yes, I went there last year.
3. Did you see many wild animals there?

4. Yes, I saw lions, tigers, and bears.
5. Do you know where such wild animals came from?
6. I suppose the lions and tigers came from India or Africa, but most of the bears came from Hokkaidō.
7. What animal was most interesting to you?
8. No animals were more interesting than monkeys.
9. Did you see the elephant?
10. O yes, I would not forget to see him.
11. What else did you see there?
12. I saw camels, snakes, cranes, etc.

LESSON V.

Jāne, cousin(kŭzn), lẽarnt, country(kŭn'trĭ), visit(vĭz'ĭt), taught, wrĭt'ten, tīme, fāll, ăn'swẽr.

LETTER-WRITING.

1. Jane is writing a letter to her cousin.

2. Jane is a little school-girl who has just learnt how to write a letter.

3. Her cousin lives in a far country.

4. She writes all about her school.

5. She says how she wishes to visit the country where her cousin lives.

6. It is quite a long letter, and a very interesting one too.

7. Do you know how to write a letter?

8. Yes, papa taught me how to write a letter.

9. Have you ever written a letter to any one?

10. Yes, I have written to my uncle several times.

11. I hope you will write to me when you can.

12. Yes, I will.   But, when I do, you must not fail to answer me.

LESSON VI.

bĕd, gēēs̶e̶, dŭc̶ks, pŏnd, mŏn′ūmĕnt, lāt̶e̶, wạr, stăt′ū̶e̶, generals(j̆ĕn′ẽrŭls), bu̶ĭld′ĭng, mu̶s̶e̶′ŭm, lī′brărȳ, among(ȧmŭng′), pleasant(plĕz′ŭnt), paths(pȧt̶hz), view(vū).

THE PARK.

1. This is a very large as well as beautiful park.

2. What a pretty flower bed that is!

3. Many geese and ducks are swimming in the pond.
4. Here is a monument of the late war.
5. There is the statue of one of our great generals.

6. This building is a museum, and that is a library.
7. Let us take a walk among the trees.
8. These are very pleasant paths.

9. I am a little tired of walking, aren't you?

10. Let us sit down on this bench.

11. What a fine view this is!

12. It is just like a picture.

LESSON VII.

addition(ăddĭsh′ŭn), subtraction(sŭbtrăk′shŭn), forty(fạr′tĭ), sĭx′tў, eighty(ā′tĭ), sĕv′ệntў, ădḍ, dollars(dŏl′lẽrs), sŭbtrăct′.

ADDITION AND SUBTRACTION.

1. Four and six make ten.

2. Thirteen and twenty-five make thirty-eight.

3. Fifty-seven and forty-three make one hundred.

4. Twenty-nine, sixty-two, and eighty-one make one hundred and seventy-two.

5. If you add thirty-five apples to seventy-eight apples, how many apples will you have?

6. We shall have one hundred and thirteen apples.

7. Suppose you had two hundred and fifty-six dollars, and you have got eighty-seven dollars more; how many dollars have you now?

8. We have three hundred and forty-three dollars.

9. If I subtract six from fourteen, eight will be left.

10. Suppose there were six hundred children in the school, and one hundred and forty-seven had been graduated; how many children would be left in the school?

11. Four hundred and fifty-three.

LESSON VIII.

relation(rēlā'shŭn), ĕld'ĕst, engaged(ĕngājd'), business(bĭz'nĕs), ĕld'ẽr, lạw, àlīvẹ', dĕạd, since(sĭns), chīld, grạndmother(grănd'mŭthẽr), grănd'fäthẽr.

RELATIONS.

1. Have you brothers and sisters?

2. Yes, I have three brothers and one sister.

3. Are you the eldest?

4. No, I am the youngest but one.

5. Who is the youngest?

6. My sister is the youngest.

7. My eldest brother is now engaged in business.

8. One of my elder brothers has just started for England, where he expects to study law.

9. Are your parents both alive?

15

10. My mother is still alive, but my father is dead.

11. How long is it since your father died?

12. He died more than ten years ago, when I was still a little child.

13. My grandmother died only a few years ago, but I do not remember my grandfather.

14. I have many uncles and aunts, of all of whom I am very fond.

LESSON IX.

stēₐm′ẽr, rough(rŭf), stormy(stₐrm′ĭ), sāfℓ, stẽrn, bōₐrd, anxious(ănk′shŭs), lănd, ŭpsĕt′, you've(yo͞ov), ĕxpē′rĭĕnçℓ, voyage(voi′ₐj), Formosa(fₐrmō′sₐ), sēₐ′sĭçk.

THE STEAMER.

1. A large steamer is on the rough sea.

2. The weather is stormy, but the steamer is safe.
3. The steamer has a Japanese flag at the stern.
4. Many passengers are on board the steamer.

5. They must be anxious to land.
6. If the steamer were smaller than it is, it would surely be upset.
7. Have you ever been on board a steamer?
8. Yes, several times.
9. I hope you've never experienced a rough voyage.

10. When I went to Formosa it was very stormy.
11. Were you sea-sick then?
12. Yes, a little.

LESSON X.

dĭrĕct'lў, ŭpŏn', ẽạrth, grōw, wẹâr, clōthẹṣ, vacation(vākā'shŭn), cities(sĭt'ēs), sēạ'-shōrẹ, sēạ'-wạtẽr, bāth'ĭng, rĕtīrẹ', vā'rĭọus, vĭl'lăḡēs, ȧvoid', hēạt, spĕnd, accompany(ăkkŭm'pȧnĭ), plăn.

SUMMER.

1. Summer is the warmest season of the year.
2. In summer the sun shines most directly upon the earth.
3. It is in summer that the trees and grass grow rapidly.
4. People wear thin clothes in summer.

5. School-children have a long vacation in this season.
6. Some of the people of large cities go to the sea-shore and enjoy sea-water bathing.

7. Others retire to various mountain villages and avoid the heat.
8. How are you going to spend your summer vacation this year?
9. I think I shall visit my uncle in Hokkaidō.

10. I wish I could accompany you.
11. What is your plan for the summer.
12. I expect to stay at home.

LESSON XI.

dĭf'fĭcŭlt, language(lăn'gwĭj), nā'tĭvĕ, flū'ĕntlў, pronunciation(prŏnŭnsĭā'shŭn), talked(tạkt), Englishman(ĭn'glĭshmŭn), ēạ'sў, ĕxprĕss', mӯsĕlf', ēạ'sĭẽr, ŭndẽrstănd', twĭçĕ, grammar(grăm'mẽr), răth'ẽr, bĕgĭn'nĭng, become(bĕkŭm'), más'tẽr.

ENGLISH STUDY.

1. I have been learning English for two years and a half.
2. Do you find it a very difficult language?
3. Yes, I do. It is so different from my native language.

4. Can you speak it quite fluently?

5. No, not yet. Pronunciation is the most difficult part of English study.

6. Have you ever talked with an Englishman or an American?

7. Yes, but it is not very easy for me to express myself in English.

8. Is it easier for you to understand than to speak English?

9. O yes, it is twice as easy.

10. How do you find English grammer?

11. It seems to be rather easy in the beginning, but the more we study it, the more difficult it becomes.

12. I hope you will soon master the language.

LESSON XII.

fōōd, order(ạr'dẽr), vĕġ'ĕtȧblẹs, mēȧt, foreigner(fŏr'ĭnẽr), seldom(sĕl'dŭm), use(yōōz), brĕȧd, wheȧt, cōld, cǫŭn'trịēs, bŏd'ịēs, clī'mȧtẹ, nĕç'ĕssȧry̆, sūịt'ȧblẹ, require(rĕkwīr').

FOOD.

1. Animals have to eat in order to live.
2. If we do not eat, we shall die.
3. There are many different kinds of food.
4. We eat rice, fish, vegetables, and some meat.
5. Foreigner eat more meat and less fish than the Japanese people.
6. Foreigners seldom eat rice, but use bread, which is made from wheat.
7. In cold countries people must eat much meat that they may keep their

bodies warm.

8. Where the climate is warm, meat is not very necessary, but vegetables are suitable.

9. Our food should not be of one kind all the time.

10. Different parts of our bodies require different kind of food.

11. We must not eat too much at a time.

LESSON XIII.

London(lŭn'dŭn), scēne, strēets, city(sĭt'ĭ), world(wûrld), royal(roi'ŭl), păl'ăçēs, government(gŭv'ẽrnmĕnt), pär'lĭȧmĕnt, St.(sānt), Pa͟͏ul's, cathedral(kāthē'drŭl), Wĕstmĭn'stẽr, abbey(ăb'bĭ), Brĭt'ĭsh, tower(tou'ẽr), wonderful(wŭn'dẽrfoͦol), spĕç'ĭmĕns, architecture(är'kĭtĕktŭr), appearance(ăppēr'ŭns), grȩāt'lў, sûrprīşę', rā͟il'rōȧds, trăm, a͟u͏tōmō'bĭlę, realize(rē'ŭlīz).

LONDON.

1. This is the scene of the streets of London.
2. London is the capital of England, and is the largest city in the world.

3. London has many grand, beautiful buildings.
4. The Royal Palaces, the Government Buildings, the Houses of Parliament, St. Paul's Cathedral,

Westminster Abbey, the British Museum, the Tower, London Bridge, etc. are wonderful specimens of architecture.

5. If you should go to London, not only those grand, beautiful buildings, but the general appearance of the streets would greatly surprise you.

6. The railroads, the tram cars, the automobiles and all would make you realize how busy the people of London are.

LESSON XIV.

somebody(sŭm′bŏdĭ), knŏċk′ĭng, Jōnĕs, ȧsk, cärd, glăd, excellent(ĕks′ĕlĕnt), prĕṣ′ĕnt, Kȧmȧkurȧ, acquaintance(ȧkwān′tŭns), hẽȧrd, husband(hŭz′bŭnd), cŭp, tēȧ.

CALLING ON A FRIEND.

1. Somebody is knocking.

2. Is Mr. Jones at home?
3. Yes, sir; but may I ask your name?
4. This is my card.
5. Walk in, if you please.

6. Please sit by the fire.
7. I am very glad to see you in such excellent health.
8. It is very kind of you to call on me.

9. I hope you are not working so hard now as you used to.

10. My work is very light at present.

11. I wonder if you can come and spend a week in my house at Kamakura.

12. This is my wife.

13. I am very happy to make your acquaintance.

14. I have heard so much of you from my husband.

15. Will you have a cup of tea?

16. Thank you.

17. Well, I must be going.

18. Please come again.

LESSON XV.

multiplication(mŭltĭplĭkā'shŭn), division (dĭvĭzh'ŭn), mŭl'tĭplīĕd, mŭl'tĭplȳ, prŏd'uct, ninety(nīn'tĭ), dĭvīd'ĕd, dĭvīdḗ', pound, equally(ē'kwŭllĭ), pẽr'sǫn, rĕçēįvḗ', lŏst, gāįn, total(tō'tŭl), sŭm.

MULTIPLICATION AND DIVISION.

1. Three times two is six.

2. Twelve multiplied by thirteen is one hundred and fifty-six.

3. If you multiply seventy-four by eight, what will be the product?

4. It is five hundred and ninety-two.

5. Suppose there were forty-five students in the class, and each student had four books; how many books would there be in the class?

6. One hundred and eighty books, in all.

7. Twenty-seven divided by three is nine.

8. If you divide forty-eight by six, you will get eight.

9. If twelve hundred pounds be equally divided among twenty-four persons, each person will receive fifty pounds.

10. Suppose I had one hundred yen, of which I lost twenty-five yen, but soon gained one hundred and fifty yen more; and the total sum was equally divided among my five children.

11. Then, each child must have received forty-five yen.

LESSON XVI.

hōtĕl′, ŭnŏc′cŭpīĕd, rĕġ′ĭstẽr, noisy(noi′zĭ), altogether(ạltōōgĕth′ẽr), vacant(vā′kŭnt), sūịt, exactly(ĕgzăkt′lĭ), chärġẹ, shĭl′lĭng, pōr′tẽr, brĭng, dĭn′nẽr, bẽtwēẹn′, past, căb.

THE HOTEL.

1. Have you a first-class room unoccupied?

2. Yes, sir. We have two or three

very good rooms.   Will you kindly register your name?

3.   How long do you expect to stay in this hotel?

4.   For a week or so.

5.   Please come this way.   How do you like this room?

6.   This room is so dark, and also very noisy, as it is close to the street.

7.   This is altogether too large a room for me.   I wonder if you have a vacant room facing the garden.

8.   This room suits me exactly.   How much a week do you charge for it?

9.   Two pounds ten shillings.

10.   All right.   Tell the porter to bring my baggage up here.

11.   At what time can I have dinner?

12.   Between half-past six and eight

o'clock.

13. I want a cab in twenty minutes.
Will you get it ready?

14. Very well, sir.

LESSON XVII.

shŏp, gentleman(jĕn'tlmŭn), quality(kwŏl'ĭtĭ),
stȳlè, prīçè, çĕnt, shĭrt, dra̤w'ērs,
nĕc̨k'tīè, chēa̤p, ga̤y̧, quī'ĕt, dozen(dŭzn),
collar(kŏl'lēr), pâįr, cŭfs, anything(ĕn'ĭthĭng),
nothing(nŭth'ĭng), to-day(to͞odā'), ō̤w̧e,
nōtè, receipt(rēsēt'), chāngè.

AT THE SHOP.

1. Good morning, sir. What can I
do for you?

2. I want a hat of good quality.

3. This is just the one you want. It
is the latest style.

4. What is the price of it?

5. Only one dollar and seventy-five cents.
6. Show me some shirts and drawers.
7. Yes, sir. These are the best we have got in our shop.
8. I'll take three of each.
9. How do you like these neckties, which are very cheap for the quality?

10. They are all too gay for me. I wish you had some of a more quiet colour.
11. Give me a dozen collars and six

pair of cuffs.

12. Very well, sir. Anything else?

13. No, nothing else to-day. How much do I owe you?

14. Eleven dollars and forty cents.

15. Here you are—a twenty-dollar note.

16. Thank you, sir. Here is our receipt, and your change, eight dollars and sixty cents.

17. All right. Good-bye!

18. Good-bye! Come again!

LESSON XVIII.

clŏçk, agrēè', ănóth'ẽr, ẁrŏng, Ẹū'rōpè, iose(loōz), īdē'à, tōld, Switzerland (swĭts'ẽrlŭnd), Swĭss, whĕth'ẽr, pāy, bĭrth'dāȳ.

THE CLOCKS AND THE WATCH.

1. Can you tell me what time it is now?

2. These clocks do not agree with one another.

3. The first clock shows that it is twenty minutes past eight o'clock.

4. It is a quarter to nine by the second clock.

5. The third one is half-past eight.

6. I think they are all wrong.

7. The right time is 8.35.

8. This is my silver watch, which my uncle gave me when he came back from Europe.

9. This watch always tells the right time.

10. It never gains nor loses.

11. Where do you think this watch was made?

12. I have no idea.

13. Uncle told me that it was made in Switzerland.

14. My watch is an American make.

15. I prefer a Swiss watch to an American watch.

16. If a watch always tells the right time, it is a good watch, whether Swiss or American.

17. How much did you pay for this watch?

18. Nothing at all; for it was a birthday present.

LESSON XIX.

mēạl, bĕlḷ, rŭng, cärvę, sẽrvę, plātę, năp′kĭn, soil, spĭlḷ, măn′nẽrs, fork(fạrk), soup(sōōp), spōōn, ḳnīfę, pōtā′tōęs, any(ĕn′ĭ), cākę, cŏf′fēę, music(mū′zĭk).

A MEAL.

1. The dinner-bell has rung.

2. Father, mother, grandmother, and all the children are at table.
3. We must not sit too close to the table nor too far away from it.

4. There are many good things on the table.
5. Father carves the meat and serves it in plates.
6. Napkins are used that we may not soil our clothes when we spill anything.
7. A man of good manners does not make much noise while eating.
8. You eat meat with your fork, and soup with your spoon ; but you must not eat anything with your knife.
9. Shall I help you to some more meat and potatoes ?
10. Not any more, thank you.
11. Which will you take, fruit or cakes?
12. I will thank you for an apple.
13. Tea and coffee are served by mother.

14. When dinner is over we leave the table and go to another room.

15. Let us have some music.

LESSON XX.

dāĭ'lў, pro'grăm, us'ually(yōō'zhŭŭlli), wĭn'tēr, bȧth, hĕȧlth'ў, breakfast(brĕk'fŭst), gymnastic(jĭmnăs'tĭk), exercise(ĕx'ērsīz), nōtᵬ'bŏŏk, luncheon(lŭnch'ŭn), commence(kŏmmĕns'), hour, nōōn, ȧftērnōōn', prĕpȧrā'tion. lĕs'sǫn.

THE DAILY PROGRAM.

1. At what time do you usually get up?

2. In summer I get up at five o'clock, but in winter I do not get up before half-past six.

3. What is the first thing you do when you have got up?

4. I take a cold bath, which I find very healthy.

5. Then comes your breakfast, I suppose?

6. Not yet, for I take a short gymnastic exercise.

7. How long does it take you to go through the exercise?

8. It does not take me more than five minutes.

9. What do you do after breakfast?

10. I get ready to go to school.

11. What do you take along with you to school?

12. I carry in my bag books, pencils, pens, note-books, paper, and luncheon.

13. At what time do the classes commence?

14. At 8 a.m.

15. How much time have you for luncheon?

16. One hour—from noon to 1 p.m.

17. I come back from school between three and four in the afternoon.

18. We take dinner at 7 o'clock.

19. After dinner I make preparations for the next day's lessons or write letters to my friends.

20. At ten o'clock I go to bed.

LESSON XXI.

wïthout', ē'vẹn, blossom(blŏs'sŭm), dressed(drĕst), gär'mĕnt, dăz'zlĭng, frō'zẹn, skātẹ, skāt'ĭng, ice(īs), hẹart'ĭlÿ, thĕmsĕlvẹs', härd'lÿ, fïrẹ'sīdẹ, comfortable(kŭm'fẽrtȧbl), hēȧt'ĕd, old-fashioned(ōld-fȧsh'ŭnd), fïrẹ'plȧçẹ, hōmẹ'līkẹ.

WINTER.

1. Winter has come at last.
2. In winter we have short days and long nights.
3. As it is very cold, we wear thick, warm clothes.

4. Most of the trees are without leaves, but when it snows they look very beautiful—even more beautiful than when they have blossoms.

5. The fields, the hills, the houses and all are dressed with pure white garments.

6. When the sun shines upon the snow it is very bright and dazzling.

7. The rivers and the ponds are frozen up so hard that children can skate there.

8. The children enjoy skating on the ice as heartily as if they did not feel the cold at all.

9. The old people shut themselves up in the house and can hardly leave the fireside.

10. Nothing is more comfortable in winter than a fire.

11. Our rooms can be heated in many different ways, but the old-fashioned fireplace is most homelike.

LESSON XXII.

measure(mĕzh′ŭr), hĕight(hīt), ĭnch′ēs, thought(thạt), tạll′ẽr, pōlẹ, yärd, equal(ē′kwŭl), rŏd, thousand(thou′zŭnd), capacity(kȧpăs′ĭtĭ), pĭtch′ẽr, quạrt, pīnt, gill(jĭl), gallon(găl′un), pĕck, bushel(boŏsh′ĕl), thẽrẹ′fōrẹ.

MEASURES.

1. What is your height?
2. I am four feet and three inches.
3. I thought you were taller than that.
4. How long do you think this pole is?
5. It must be at least seven yards long.
6. How many feet make a yard?
7. Three feet make a yard.
8. How many inches are there in a foot?

9. There are twelve inches in a foot.

10. A yard is then equal to thirty-six inches.

11. What is a rod?

12. A rod is five yards and a half, that is, sixteen feet and a half.

13. How many rods are there in a mile?

14. Three hundred and twenty rods, that is, five thousand two hundred and eighty feet.

---

15. What is the capacity of this pitcher?

16. Its capacity is a quart and a half.

17. How much is a quart?

18. A quart is two pints or eight gills.

19. How many quarts of milk make a gallon?

45

20. Four quarts make a gallon.

21. How many quarts of wheat make a peck?

22. Eight quarts make a peck, and four pecks make a bushel.

23. A bushel is, therefore, thirty-two quarts, that is, sixty-four pints.

LESSON XXIII.

Sŭn'dā͑, nāmḙ'lў̆, Monday(mŭn'dă̆), Tuesday(tūz'dă̆), Wednesday(wĕnz'dă̆), Thursday(thûrz'dă̆), Frĭ'dā͑, Săt'ûrdā͑, wēḙk'dā͑, rĕcrēa'tion, plāçḙ, ȧmūṣḙ'mĕnt, sufficient(sŭffĭsh'ĕnt), energy(ĕn'ẽrjĭ), appreciate(ăpprē'shĭāt), hŏl'ĭdā͑, throughout(thrōōout'), sure(shōōr), ĭn'jŭrḙ, ŭnā'blḙ.

THE DAYS OF THE WEEK.

1. What is the first day of the week called?

2. It is called Sunday.

3. How many more days are there in the week?

4. Six more; namely, Monday, Tuesday, Wednesday, Thursday Friday, and Saturday.

5. These six days are called weekdays.

6. On Sunday we have no school and can go out into the fields for recreation.

7. We ought not to study or do any work on that day.

8. Many people go to parks and visit museums or other places of amusement.

9. Boys play ball or take a long walk on Sunday.

10. On weekdays we go to school and learn many things there.

11. If We did not take recreation on Sunday, we should not have sufficient energy to go through the work on weekdays.

12. We can appreciate Sunday after the hard work on weekdays.

13. Some people work on Sunday as hard as on weekdays, so that they have no holiday throughout the year.

14. They may think they can do more work than others.

15. But such people are sure to injure their health, and become unable to work.

16. In the long run, therefore, they cannot do so much work as those who take recreation on Sunday.

LESSON XXIV.

emperor(ĕm′pẽrẽr), national(năsh′ŭnŭl), celebrate(sĕl′ĕbrāt), Nŏvĕm′bẽr, mĭl′ĭtărў, review(rĕvū′), hĭmsĕlf′, trōops, ŭnlĕss′, prĕvĕnt′ĕd, ŭnȧvoid′ȧblĕ, official(ŏffĭsh′ŭl), nōblĕ, foreign(fŏr′ĭn), ambassador (ămbăs′ȧdûr), mĭn′ĭstẽr, păl′ȧçĕ, congrăt′ūlātĕ, aч′dĭĕnçĕ, invītĕ′, fēȧst, ăffâįr′, dĭstĭn′guĭshĕd, Tōkyō, Yokohȧmȧ, Kĭmĭ-gȧ-yo, voiçĕ.

THE EMPEROR'S BIRTHDAY.

1. Do you know how many national holidays we have?
2. I think we have ten.
3. Why do we celebrate the third of November?
4. Because it is the Emperor's birthday.
5. What takes place on this national holiday?

6. A military review takes place on that day.
7. Does the Emperor himself review the troops?

8. O yes, he does it in person, unless he is prevented by something unavoidable.
9. On this day all high officials, nobles, and foreign ambassadors and ministers go to the Palace to con-

gratulate the Emperor.

10. The Emperor receives them in audience and invites them to the feast.

11. On the evening of that day, the Minister of Foreign Affairs gives a ball to the distinguished foreigners as well as natives who are in Tōkyō and Yokohama.

12. Long live the Emperor!

13. Let us sing " Kimi-ga-yo " at the top of our voice.

LESSON XXV.

Jăn'ŭărў, Fĕb'rŭărў, März, Ā'prĭl, Măў, Jūnἔ, July(jŭlī'), Aŭ'gŭst, Sĕptĕm'bẽr, Octō'bẽr, Dĕçĕm'bẽr, plănt, bĕgĭn', chĕr'rў, hot, ĕxcûr'sion, spring, aŭ'tŭmἡ, ĕxçĕpt', lēἃp'-yēἃr.

THE MONTHS AND SEASONS.

1. A year has twelve months.

2. They are January, February, March, April, May, June, July, August, September, October, November, and December.
3. January is the first month of the year, and its first day is called New Year's Day.
4. February is one of the coldest months, if not the coldest.
5. In March the plants begin to grow.
6. In April cherry blossoms are beautiful.
7. May is a very pleasant month.
8. The warm season begins in June.
9. In July and August school-children have a long vacation, for it is then too hot for them to study.
10. In September schools are open again.

11. October is the best month for an excursion.
12. In November we have two national holidays.
13. December is the last month of the year and the beginning of the cold season.
14. A year is divided into four seasons, —spring, summer, autumn, and winter.
15. Spring is March, April, and May; summer is June, July, and August; autumn is September, October, and November; and winter is December, January, and February.
16. April, June, September, and November have each thirty days.
17. February has twenty-eight days, except in a leap-year when it has

53

twenty-nine days.

18. The other months have each thirty-
one days.

LESSON XXVI.

măp, ĕm'pīrę̆, cŏnsĭst', Hŏnshū, Shikoku,
Kyūshū, Saghalin(sägälēn'), island(ĭ'lŭnd),
inclūd'ing, Loō'choo, Kurile(koō'rĭl),
group(groōp), ĕxtĕnd', north(nạrth),
south, ĕxtrēmę̆'lў, centre(sĕn'tĕr), fā'mọ̆ŭs,
Tonĕ, Shĭnáno, Kĭso, trăv'ĕllĕr, Kyōto,
Nárà, commercial(kŏmmẽr'shŭl), ábound',
tropical(trŏp'ĭkŭl), rĕ̇spĕct'.

THE MAP OF JAPAN.

1. This is the map of Japan.
2. The Empire of Japan consists of
Honshū, Shikoku, Kyūshū,
Hokkaidō, Formosa, one half of
Saghalin, and about four thousand
small islands, including the Loochoo

and Kurile groups.

3. The empire extends from north to south over many thousand miles.

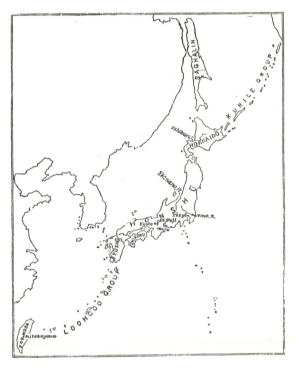

4. It is very cold in Saghalin and the Kurile islands, while it is extremely warm in Formosa.

5. Tōkyō, the capital of Japan, is about in the centre of Honshū.

6. Niitakayama, the highest mountain in the Japanese Empire, is in Formosa.

7. Mount Fuji is next in height, but far more famous than Niitakayama.

8. The Shinano, The Ishikari, and the Tone are the three greatest rivers in Japan.

9. Have you travelled a great deal in Japan?

10. Yes, but I have not been to Saghalin yet.

11. No cities in Japan are more interesting to travellers than Kyōto and Nara.

12. Ōsaka is the largest commercial city in this country.

13. Formosa abounds with tropical plants and fruits.

14. Hokkaidō is like North America in many respects.

LESSON XXVII.

coŭp'lĕ, stămp, weigh(wā), pōst'āġĕ, momme, ordinary(ar'dĭnărĭ), pōst'-cärd, rĕtûrn', sĕnd, pär'çĕl, dĕṣīrĕ', w̖răp, căsh, postal(pōst'ŭl), rĕmĭt'tĕr, ăddrĕss', sīg̑n, tĕl'ĕgrăm, pŏs'sĭblĕ, clĕrk, wĭn'dōw̖, telephone(tĕl'ĕfōn), ĕv'ĕrỹ, No.(nŭm'bĕr).

THE POST-OFFICE.

1. I want a couple of three-sen stamps and a ten-sen stamp.

2. Please weigh this letter and tell me what the postage will be.

3. It weighs five momme, and the postage is six sen.

4. Will you give me ten ordinary

post-cards and three foreign post-cards?
5. I should like to have a return post-card too.
6. I want to have this letter registered.

7. All right; ten sen please.
8. Do you want to send this by parcel post?
9. Yes, but how much have I to pay for it?

10. Which do you want, the ordinary parcel post or the registered parcel post?

11. The registered parcel post, if you please.

12. You will have to pay twenty-four sen for it then.

13. By the way, you must wrap up your parcel in oil paper or some other strong paper.

14. Please cash this postal order for thirty-six yen.

15. What is the remitter's name and address?

16. Sign your name.

17. Here is a telegram which I want to send as soon as possible.

18. Put a twenty-sen stamp on it, and present it to the second clerk from

the window.

19. May I use the telephone?

20. Yes, if you pay five sen for every five minutes.

21. Please call up No. 1080 for me.

LESSON XXVIII.

gonĕ, smīlĕ, ăttrăct′ĭvĕ, welcome(wĕl′kŭm), rāçĕ, mō′mĕnt, hûrdlĕ, ȧmūş′ĭng, wĭn′nẽrs, prīz′ēs, rĕgăt′tȧ, Sumĭdȧ, excited(ĕksīt′ĕt), drạẉ, crews(krōōs), pulling(pŏŏl′ĭng), wĭn, lạẉ′rĕls, chärm′ĭng.

SPRING.

1. Winter is gone and spring is come.

2. The hills are no more covered with snow.

3. The trees and grass seem to smile.

4. Various flowers make the fields very attractive to the young and the old.

5. The sweet music of singing birds shows how glad they are to welcome spring.
6. Look at the field-day exercise of school-children.

7. A group of boys are ready to start on a foot race every moment.
8. How high he jumps with a pole!
9. The hurdle race is more amusing than anything else.

10. The winners receive various kinds of prizes and look very proud.

11. Here is a regatta on the Sumida River.

12. Thousands of people on the bank are very excited over it.

13. The regatta would not draw so many spectators but for the cherry blossoms that are now at their best.

14. The crews of those three boats are pulling their hardest.

15. Which will win the laurels? Who will get the champion flag?

16. Spring is the most charming season of the year.

17. I wish it were always spring.

LESSON XXIX.

newspaper(nūz'pāpēr), regularly(rŏg'ŭlērlĭ), regular(rĕg'ŭlēr), sŭbscrīb'ēr, York(yạrk), concerning(kŏnsērn'ĭng), election (ĕlĕk'shŭn), preṣ'ĭdĕnt, wēĕk'lў, edition(ĕdĭsh'ŭn), exceedingly(ĕksēd'ĭnglĭ), ōẁn, ĭllŭs'trātĕd, Graphic(grăf'ĭk), magazines(măgȧzēns'), lend.

THE NEWSPAPER.

1. What newspaper are you reading now?

2. I am reading "The Japan Times"

3. Do you take in that paper regularly?

4. Yes, I am a regular subscriber to it.

5. Is there anything new in this morning's paper?

6. No, nothing but a telegram from New York concerning the election of the President.

7. Do you read any English or American paper?

8. Yes, I read the weekly edition "The London Times" but no American paper.

9. It must be very interesting to read foreign papers and learn what is going on in other countries.

10. But I am exceedingly sorry that I am unable to read any language but my own.

11. Look at these papers, which I know you can understand even if you don't know English.

12. Well, I see they are full of very fine pictures.

13. This illustrated paper is called "The Graphic".

14. I wish we had such good illustrated

papers in Japan.

15. I hope the day will soon come when our country will abound with good newspapers and magazines.

16. Will you lend me some of these illustrated papers for a day or two?

17. Certainly, you may take them home and show them to your brothers and sisters.

18. I am greatly obliged to you.

LESSON XXX.

fârẹwĕll', final(fī'nŭl), examinations (ĕgzămĭna'shŭns), passed(past), successfully(sŭksĕs'fōolĭ), grădŭā'tion, ceremony(sĕr'ĕmōnĭ), hĕld, certificates (sẽrtĭf'ĭkāts), clàss'màtẹs, ĕn'tẽr, grādẹs, mĕm'bẽrs, ăpprĕn'tĭçēs, plăn'nĭng, abrǫad', līkẹ'lў, nēẹd, dèạr, beloved(bĕlŭv'ĕd), fēẹl, pẽrhăps', ablẹ, future(fū'chὔr), correspondence(kŏrĕspŏnd'ĕns).

FAREWELL.

1. The final examinations are over at last.
2. We have all passed the examinations successfully.
3. The graduation ceremony is to be held in a week.
4. How happy we shall be when we receive our certificates!
5. We have been together in the same school and in the same class for nine years.
6. But we are now to part with one another.
7. We must have our class picture taken.
8. Some of our classmates expect to enter schools of higher grades.
9. Several members of our class will

become clerks or apprentices.

10. At least two of them are planning to go abroad—very likely to America.

11. Many of them will go home to live with their parents, who need their help in many ways.

12. Farewell, our dear old school! We will come and see you now and then.

13. Farewell, our beloved teachers! We shall never forget how good and kind you have been to us.

14. Farewell, dear classmates! It makes us feel sad to think that we shall perhaps never be able to get together in the future.

15. Let us keep up a correspondence.

16. As I will surely answer your letters, you must never fail to answer mine.

GLOSSARY.

a,	abbey,	able,
abound,	about,	abroad,
accompany,	acquaintance,	add,
addition,	address,	affair,
Africa,	after,	afternoon,
again,	ago,	agree,
alive,	all,	also,
altogether,	always,	am,
ambassador,	America,	American,
among,	amusement,	amusing,
an,	and,	animal,
another,	answer,	anxious,
any,	anything,	appearance,
apple,	appreciate,	apprentice,
April,	architecture,	are,
aren't,	arithmetic,	as,
ask,	at,	attractive,
audience,	August,	aunt,
automobile,	autumn,	avoid,
away,	back,	bag,

baggage,	ball (tama),	ball (yakwai),
bank,	bath,	bathing,
be,	bear (n.),	beautiful,
because,	become,	bed,
been,	before (prep.),	begin,
beginning,	bell,	beloved,
bench,	best,	better,
between,	big,	bird,
birthday,	blossom,	board,
boat,	bodies,	book,
both,	boy,	bread,
breakfast,	bridge,	bright,
bring,	British,	brother,
building,	bushel,	business,
busy,	but (conj.),	but (prep.),
by,	cab,	cake,
call,	came,	camel,
can,	cannot,	can't,
capacity,	capital,	car,
card,	carry,	carve,
cash,	catch,	cathedral,

celebrate,
ceremony,
champion,
charles,
check,
children,
city,
clear,
clock,
coffee,
colour,
coming,
concerning,
correspondence,
country,
cover,
cuffs,
dark,
dead,
December,
die,

cent,
certainly,
change (tsuri),
charming,
cherry,
chimney,
class,
clerk,
close (adj.),
cold,
come,
commence,
congratulate,
could,
couple,
crane,
cup,
day,
deal,
desire,
different,

centre,
certificate,
change (v.),
cheap,
child,
cities,
classmate,
climate,
clothes,
collar,
comfortable,
commercial,
consist,
countries,
cousin,
crew,
daily,
dazzling,
dear,
did,
difficult,

dinner,	directly,	distinguished
divided,	division,	do,
does,	dollar,	don't,
down,	dozen,	draw,
drawer,	dressed,	duck,
each,	earth,	easier,
easy,	eat,	edition,
eight,	eighty,	elder,
eldest,	election,	elephant,
eleven,	else,	emperor,
empire,	energy,	engage,
engine,	England,	English,
Englishman,	enjoy,	enter,
equal,	equally,	Europe,
etc.,	even,	evening,
ever,	every,	exactly,
examination,	exceedingly,	excellent,
except,	excited,	excursion,
exercise,	expect,	experience (v.),
express,	extend,	extremely,
face (v.),	fail,	famous,

far,	farewell,	father,
favorite,	feast,	February,
feel,	feet,	few,
field,	field-day,	fifty,
final,	find,	fine,
fire,	fireplace,	fireside,
first,	fish,	five,
flag,	flower,	fluently,
fond,	food,	foot,
for (prep.),	for (conj.),	foreign,
foreigner,	forget,	fork,
Formosa,	forty,	fourteen,
Friday,	friend,	from,
frozen,	fruit,	Fuji,
funnel,	future,	gain, (v.),
gallon,	garden,	garment,
gave,	gay,	geese,
general, (adj.),	general, (n.),	gentleman,
geography,	get,	gill,
girl,	glad,	go,
gone,	good,	good-bye,

got,	government,	grade,
graduation,	graduated,	grammar,
grand,	grandfather,	grandmother,
Graphic,	grass,	great,
greatly,	ground,	group,
grow,	gymnastic,	had,
half,	hallo,	happy,
hard,	hardly,	has,
hat,	have,	haven't,
he,	health,	healthy,
heard,	heartily,	heat,
heated,	height,	held,
help,	Henry,	her,
here,	high,	hill,
him,	himself,	history,
Hokkaidō,	holiday,	home,
homelike,	Honshū,	hope,
hot,	hotel,	hour,
house,	how,	hundred,
hurdle,	husband,	I,
ice,	idea,	if,

illustrated,	in,	inches,
including,	India,	injure (v.),
interesting,	invite,	is,
Ishikari,	island,	it,
its,	Jane,	January,
Japan,	Japanese,	Jennie,
Jones,	July,	jump,
June,	just,	Kamakura,
keep,	kind (adj.),	kind (n.),
kindly,	knife,	knocking,
know,	Kurile,	Kyōto,
Kyūshū,	land,	language,
large,	last,	late,
laurels,	law,	leap-year,
learn,	learnt,	least,
leave (v.),	leaves (n.),	left,
lend,	less,	lesson,
let,	letter (tegami),	letter-writing,
library,	light (n.),	light (adj.),
like (adj.),	like (v.),	likely,
lion,	little,	live,

London,	long,	Loochoo,
look,	lose,	lost,
love,	low,	luncheon,
made,	magazine,	make (v.),
make (n.),	man,	manners,
many,	map,	March,
master (v.),	may (aux.),	May (gogatsu),
me,	meal,	measure,
meat,	member,	mile,
military,	milk,	mine,
minister,	minute,	moment,
momme,	Monday,	monkey,
month,	monument,	more,
morning,	most,	mother,
mount,	mountain,	Mr.,
much,	multiplication,	multiplied,
multiply,	museum,	music,
must,	my,	myself,
name,	namely,	napkin,
Nara,	national,	native,
necessary,	necktie,	need,

never,

next,

night,

no,

noise,

nor,

note (satsu),

November,

O,

October,

official (n.),

old-fashioned,

one (pron.),

or,

Ōsaka,

our,

owe,

palace,

parcel,

parliament,

pass,

new,

nicely,

nine,

No.,

noisy,

north,

note-book,

now,

oblige,

of,

oil,

on,

only,

order,

other,

out,

own,

papa,

parents,

part (v.),

passenger,

newspaper,

Niitakayama,

ninety,

noble (n.),

noon,

not,

nothing,

now-a-days,

o'clock,

off,

old,

one (adj.),

open (adj.),

ordinary,

ought,

over,

pair,

paper,

park,

part (n.),

past,

path,	Paul,	pay,
peck,	pen,	pencil,
penknives,	people,	perhaps,
person,	picture,	pint,
pitcher,	place,	plan,
planning,	plant,	plate,
play,	pleasant,	please,
pole,	pond,	porter,
possible,	postage,	postal,
post-card,	post-office,	potatoes,
pound,	prefer,	preparation,
present (n.),	present (adj.),	present (v.),
president,	pretty,	prevent,
price,	prize,	product,
program,	pronunciation,	proud,
pull,	pure,	put,
quality,	quart,	quarter,
quiet,	quite,	race (kyōsō),
railroad,	rapidly,	rather,
reading,	ready,	realize,
receipt,	receive,	recreation,

regatta, register, regular,
regularly, relation, remember,
remittar, require, respect,
retire, return, review,
rice, right, river,
rod, room, rough,
royal, run (n.), rung,
running, sad, safe,
Saghalin, same, Saturday,
saw (past), say, scene,
school, sea, sea-shore,
sea-sick, season, seat,
see-water, second (adj.), see,
seem, seldom, sell,
sen, send, September,
serve, seven, seventy,
several, shall, she,
Shikoku, shilling, Shinano,
shine, shirt, shop,
short, should, show,
shut, side, sign,

silver,	since,	sing,
sir,	sister,	sit,
six,	sixty,	skate,
skating,	small,	smile,
smoke,	snake,	snow (n.),
snow (v.),	so,	soil (v),
some,	somebody,	something,
soon,	sorry,	soup,
south,	speak,	specimen,
spectator,	spend,	spill,
spoon,	spring (haru),	St.,
stamp,	start,	station,
statue,	stay,	steamer,
stern,	still,	stomach,
stormy,	street,	strong,
student,	study (n.),	study (v.),
style,	subscriber,	subtract,
subtraction,	successfully,	such,
sufficient,	suit (v.),	suitable,
sum,	Sumida,	summer,
sun,	Sunday,	suppose,

sure,	surely,	surprise,
sweet,	swimming,	Swiss,
Switzerland,	table,	take,
taken,	talk,	taller,
taught,	tea,	teacher,
telegram,	telephone,	tell,
ten,	than,	thank,
that (adj.),	that (conj.),	the,
their,	them,	themselves,
then,	there,	therefore,
these,	they,	thick,
thin,	thing,	think,
third,	thirteen,	thirty,
this,	those,	thought (past),
thousand,	three,	through,
throughout,	Thursday,	ticket,
tiger,	time,	times,
tired,	to,	to-day,
together,	Tōkyō,	told,
Tone,	too (mata),	too (amari),
top,	total,	tower,

train,	tram,	travel,
traveller,	tree,	troops,
tropical,	trouble,	Tuesday,
twelve,	twenty,	twice,
two,	Ueno,	unable,
unavoidable,	uncle,	understand,
unless,	unoccupied,	up,
upon,	upset,	us,
use (v.),	used,	usually,
vacant,	vacation,	various,
vegetable,	very,	view,
village,	visit,	voice,
voyage,	walk (v.),	walk (n.),
want,	war,	was,
way,	we,	we're,
wear,	weather,	Wednesday,
week,	weekday,	weekly,
weigh,	welcome,	well (adv.),
went,	were,	Westminster,
what,	wheat,	when (inter.),
when (conj.),	where (inter),	whether,

which (inter), which (rel.), while,
white, who, whom,
why, wife, wild,
will, win, window,
winner, winter, wish,
with, without, wonder,
wonderful, work (n.), work (v.),
world, would, wrap,
writing, written, wrong,
yard, year, yen,
yes, yet, Yokohama,
York, you, young,
your, you've, zoological,

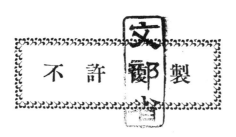

明治四十三年四月二十日印刷
明治四十三年四月二十三日發行

リーダー卷參

定價金拾錢

著作權者　文　部　省

發　行　者　株式會社 國定教科書共同販賣所
東京市日本橋區新右衛門町十六番地

代表者　大　橋　新　太　郎

印　刷　者　　　河　合　辰　太　郎
凸版印刷株式會社代表者
東京市下谷區二長町一番地

印　刷　所　　　凸版印刷株式會社
東京市下谷區二長町一番地

發　行　所　株式會社 國定教科書共同販賣所
東京市日本橋區新右衛門町十六番地

小学校用文部省英語読本巻一教授書

小學校用

文部省英語讀本

卷 一

教 授 書

文 部 省

小學校用

文部省英語讀本

卷 一

教授書

文 部 省

緒　言

本書ハ文部省英語讀本卷一ノ敎師用參考書トシテ編纂セルモノナリ該英語讀本ニヨリ英語ヲ授ケントスルモノハ次ノ諸點ニ注意センコトヲ望ム

1. 毎課ノ敎授ニ先ダチ組織的敎案ヲ作リ細密ナル順序ヲ定ムベシ

2. 敎師ノ發音ハ明瞭正確ナルヲ要ス

3. 實物又ハ圖畫ヲ用ヒテ敎授スベシ圖畫ヲ用フル際ハ讀本中ノ揷繪ト均シキ掛圖ヲ用フルヲ可トス

4. 敎授ノ際初ハ生徒ノ耳ニ由リテ學バシメ次ニ口ヲ以テ練習セシメ其ノ次ニ目ヲ以テ講讀セシメ最後ニ手ヲ以テ書キ綴ランム此ノ順序ニ從フハ極メテ肝要ニシテ敎課ヲ敎フルノ際決シテ初ヨリ讀本ヲ開カシムベカラズ

5. 新課ノ初ニ必ズ既修ノ諸課ニ就キテ復習セシムベシ

6. 復習課ニ於テハ既修ノ諸課ヲ漏ナク復習セシムベシ

7. 毎課ノ敎授ニ要スル時間ハ凡ソ二時間タルベシ

8. 生徒學力ノ程度又ハ時間ノ分量等ニヨリ敎師ハ臨機ノ變化ヲナスベシ

（ 1 ）

第　一　課

1. 教師先ヅ教壇ノ上ニ立チヘペんノ實物又ハ圖畫ヲ
全級ノ生徒ニ示シテ遺漏ナカラシム

2. 之ヲ示シナガラ教師ハ數回

Pen.

ト發音シ全級ノ生徒ヲシテ之ヲ聞知セシメ次ニ 一本ノ
ペンハ

A pen.

ト云ンコトヲ敎ヘ幾回モ其ノ發音ヲ示シ次ノ諸點ヲ敎
フ

（1）　pĕ ハ日本語ノペノ如クナルコト

（2）　n ハ日本語ノんト異ナリ舌端ヲ上顎ニ附着シテ
發音スルコト

（3）　不定冠詞ノ A ハ Ā ヨリモ寧ロ Å （日本語ノあ）
ト發音スベキコト

3. 成ルベク多數ノ生徒ヲシテ實物又ハ圖畫ニヨリ
(1) Pen (2) A pen ノ發音及ビ譯解ヲ試ミシメ若シ誤謬
アレ時ハ一々丁寧ニ之ヲ訂正ス

4. 次ニ黑板ニ

Pen.

ト書キテ文字ヲ示シ Pe ハペト讀ミ之ニ n ヲ加ヘテペ

ントナルコトヲ教フ。又

A pen.

ノ二語ヲモ並べ書キテ之ヲ示シ此ノ二語ハ幾分カ近ク續ケテ讀ムベキコトヲ知ラシム。又 P, A, e, n, p ノ五文字ノ名稱ヲ教ヘ其ノ中 P ト p トハ同字ナレドモ P ハ頭文字 p ハ小文字ナルコトヲ說明ス。而シテ此ノ際 A, と ノ發音ヲ明示シ且文章ノ結尾ニハ period (.) ヲ附シ其ノ中途ニハ Comma (,) ヲ附スルモノナルコトヲ教フベシ

五文字ノ名稱ハ次ノ如シ

A＝えーい   e＝いー

P＝びー   n＝ĕn

p＝びー

5. 此ノ五文字ノ名稱及ビ發音ト二語ノ發音及ビ譯解トノ練習ヲナサシム

6. 英字ノ書體ニ印刷體ト草書體トノ二種アルコトヲ說明シ草書體ニテ

A pen.

ノ書方ヲ教ヘ之ヲ練習セシム。又書方練習ノ爲ニ用フル文章ハ矢張讀方及ビ譯解ヲナサシムベシ

讀方ハ
　A⌒penˋ.

譯解ハ
　(一本ノ)ぺん

第　二　課

1. 復　習

　A, P.

　e, n, p.

　Ȧ, pĕn.

　Penˋ.

　A⌒penˋ.

2. 書物ノ實物又ハ圖畫ヲ全級ノ生徒ニ示シテ數回
　Book.

ト發音シ一本ノぺント一冊ノ書物トヲ示シテ
　A pen and a book.

ト發音シ次ニ一冊ノ書物ト一本ノぺんトヲ指シテ

(4)

A book and a pen.

ト發音シ幾回モ之ヲ繰返シ次ノ諸點ヲ敎フ

(1) boŏ ハ日本語ノぶノ如クナルコト

(2) book 及ビ and ノ語尾ハ く (ku) 及ビ ど (do) ニ
アラズシテ唯 k 及ビ d ノ子音ノミナルコト

(3) and ノ母音ハえニアラズあニアラズ殆ド其ノ中
間ノ ă ナルコト

3. 成ルベク多數ノ生徒ヲシテ實物又ハ圖畫ニヨリ
(1) Book (2) A pen and a book (3) A book and a
pen ノ發音及ビ譯解ヲ試ミシメ シ誤認アル時ハ一々
丁寧ニ之ヲ訂正ス

4. 次ニ黑板ニ Book 及ビ and ノ兩新語ヲ書キテ之
ヲ示シ book ノ發音ハ ぶく ニアラズシテ ぶっk ナルコ
トヲ敎フ。又

A pen and a book.

ト書キテ B ト b トハ同字ナレドモ前者ハ 頭文字ニシ
テ後者ハ小文字ナルコトヲ說キ且 あーぺん 又ハ あー
ぶっk ト讀マズシテ あぺん 又ハ あぶっk ト短ク縮メテ
讀ムベキコトヲ知ラシム。次ニ

A book and a pen.

ノ文字ヲ敎フルニモ同一ノ順序ヲ取ルベシ。而シテ最
後ニ B, o, k, a, d, b ノ六文字ノ名稱及ビ發音ヲ敎ヘ ă

(5)

及ビ ŏŏ ノ發音ヲ明示ス

六新文字ノ名稱ハ次ノ如シ

a＝えーい　　　k＝けーい

B＝b＝びー　　o＝をーう

d＝dee

5. 六新字ノ名稱及ビ發音ト二新語ノ發音 及ビ譯解
トノ練習ヲナサシメ次ニ (1) Book (2) A pen and a book
(3) A book and a pen ノ讀方及ビ譯解ヲ練習セシム

6. 書方

A pen and a book.

此ノ文章ノ讀方及ビ譯解ヲナサシムベシ

讀方ハ

A⌒pen and a⌒book'.

譯解ハ

(一本ノ)ぺんト(一冊ノ)書物ト

第 三 課

1. 復 習

A, B, P.

(6)

a, b, d, e, k, n, o, p.

Ȧ, ănd, bŏŏk, pĕn.

A⌢pen and a⌢book'.

A⌢book and a⌢pen'.

A pen and a book.

2. 大ナル書物ノ實物又ハ圖畫ヲ全級ノ生徒ニ示シテ之ヲ指サシナガラ

It is a book.

ト云ヒ又手眞似ニテ大ナル書物ノ形容ヲナシナガラ

Is it a big book?

ト問ヒ點頭キナガラ

Yes, it is a big book.

ト答フ。斯ノ如クスルコト數回ニシテ生徒ガ自カラ其ノ意ヲ悟得スルニ至ラバ極メテ幸ナレドモ若シ困難ナラバ更ニ其ノ意義ヲ說明シテ後此ノ會話ヲ繰返シ殊ニ次ノ諸點ヲ敎フ

(1) it, is, big, yes ノ語尾ハ と(to), ず(zu), ぐ(gu), す(su) ニアラズシテ唯 t, z, g, s ノ子音ナルガ故ニ いっt, いz, びっg, いぇs ナルコト

(2) it, is, big ノ母音ハ日本語ノハイト大差ナキコト

(3) yes ノ母音ハ pen ノ母音ト同ジクえナルコト

(7)

(4) y ノ音ハやいゆえよヲ發音スル時ニ於ケル口ノ形ヲナシテ發音スベキモノナレバ yes ハ yₑs ナルコト

(5) Is it a big book? ノ如キ疑問文ノ末尾ハ音調ヲ高ムベキコト及ビ他ノ文章ノ末尾ハ音調ヲ低クスベキコト

3. 成ルベク多數ノ生徒ヲシテ實物又ハ圖畫ニヨリ本課三文章ノ發音及ビ譯解ヲ試ミシメ若シ誤謬アル時ハ一々丁寧ニ之ヲ訂正ス

4. 次ニ此ノ三文章ヲ順次黑板ニ書キ反復其ノ讀方及ビ譯解ヲ敎ヘ it, big ハ いt, びg ニアラズシテ いっt, びっg ナルコト之ニ反シテ is, yes ハ いっz, えっs ニアラズシテ いz, いₑs ナルコトヲ知ラシムベシ。又 it is 及ビ is it ハ其ノ間ヲ短ク縮メテ速ニ讀ムベキコトヲ敎フ即チ

讀方ハ

(1) It⌒is a⌒book↘.

(2) Is⌒it a⌒big book↗?

(3) Yes↗, it⌒is a⌒big book↘.

譯解ハ

(1) ソレハ(一冊ノ)書物デアル

(2) ソレハ(一冊ノ)大ナル書物デアルカ

(3) 然リソレハ(一冊ノ)大ナル書物デアル

(8)

最後ニ六箇ノ新文字ノ名稱及ビ發音ヲ示シ I ト i ト
ハ同文字ナレドモ前者ハ頭文字ニシテ後者ハ小文字ナ
ルコトヲ説明シ且 I ノ發音ヲ明示シ又疑問文ノ終ニハ
interrogation mark (?) ヲ附スルコトヲ教フ

六新文字ノ名稱ハ次ノ如シ

g＝jee　　　　　t＝tee

I＝i＝あい　　　y＝わい

s＝ĕs

5. 六新字ノ名稱及ビ發音ト四新語ノ發音及ビ譯解
トノ練習ヲナサシノ次ニ本課三文章ノ讀方及ビ譯解ヲ
練習セシム

6. 書方

It is a big book.

此ノ文章ノ讀方及ビ譯解ヲナサシムベシ

讀方ハ

It⌢is a⌢big book'.

譯解ハ

ソレハ(一冊ノ)大ナル書物デアル

———————

(9)

第 四 課

l 復習

A, B, I, P, Y.

a, b, d, e, g, i, k, n, o, p, s, t.

ȧ, ănd, pĕn, bŏŏk, bĭg, ĭt, ĭṣ, yĕs.

It⌒is a⌒pen'.

Is⌒it a⌒pen'?

Yes', it⌒*is* a⌒pen'.

A⌒pen and a⌒big book'.

A book and a pen. It is a big
book.

2. 机ノ上ニ書物ヲ置キ又ハ其ノ圖ヲ示シ手眞似等
ノ助ヲ以テ

The book is on the desk.

ト云ヒ

Do you see the book?

ト問ヒ點頭キナガラ

Yes, I see it on the desk.

ト答ヘ又

(10)

I see the desk and the book.

ト云フ。斯ノ如クスルコト數回ニシテ生徒ヲシテ其ノ大意ヲ悟ラシメ更ニ各文章ノ意義ヲ說明シテ此ノ會話ヲ繰返シ次ノ諸點ヲ敎フ

(1) the ハ實際子音ノ前ニアル時ハ thŭ トナリ母音ノ前ニアル時ハ thĭ トナリ語氣ヲ强ムル爲ニ用フル時ハ thē トナルヲ以テ規則トスレドモ初學者ニ是等複雜ナルコトヲ敎フルハ不必要ナルガ故ニ先ヅ一般ニ thē トシテ敎フルヲ可ナリトス唯 th ノ音ハ日本人ニ取リテ極メテ困難ナルモノノ一ナルニ由リ舌及ビ齒ノ位置等ヲ詳シク說明シテ其ノ發音ヲ敎フベキコト

(2) ðn ノ母音モ日本語ニナキ音ナレバ明瞭ニ發音ヲ示シテ敎フベキコト

(3) desk ノ語尾ヲ すく ト云ハザル樣注意スベキコト

(4) do ヲ づー トセザル樣注意スベキコト

(5) you ハ よーう ニアラズシテ ゆー ナルコト

(6) see モ日本人ニ困難ナル音ニシテ しー(shē) トナリ勝チナレバ之ニ注意スベキコト

(7) 疑問文ノ末尾ニ於テ音調ヲ高ムルコトト非疑問文ノ末尾ニ於テ音調ヲ低クスルコト

3. 成ルベク多數ノ生徒ヲシテ實物又ハ圖畵ニヨリ

（ 11 ）

本課四文章ノ發音及ビ譯解ヲ試ミシメ若シ誤謬アル時ハ一々丁寧ニ之ヲ訂正ス

4. 次ニ此ノ四文章ヲ順次黒板ニ書キ反復其ノ讀方及ビ譯解ヲ教ヘ次ノ諸點ヲ說明ス

(1) do ハど一ニアラザルコト

(2) see ハ二箇ノ e ヲ有スレドモし一い一ニアラズシテ唯し一ナルコト

(3) I ハあいニシテあトいトノ間ヲ餘リ詰メザルコト

(4) the book, the desk, do you, see it 等ハ急速ニ續ケテ讀ムコト

(5) the ハ "彼の" ト云フ意ノ輕キモノナレド特ニ譯出スルノ必要ナキコト

(6) on ハ "上に" ト譯スベキコト

讀方ハ

(1) The⌢book is on the⌢desk`.

(2) Do⌢you see the⌢book'?

(3) Yes', I see⌢it on the⌢desk`.

(4) I see the⌢desk and the⌢book`.

譯解ハ

(1) 書物ガ机ノ上ニアル

(2) 汝ハ書物ヲ見ルカ

（3）　然リ余ハ其ノ机ノ上ニアルヲ見ル

（4）　余ハ机ト書物トヲ見ル

次ニ五箇ノ新文字ノ名稱及ビ發音ヲ示シ D, T ハ d,
t ノ頭文字ナルコトト y ハ Y ノ小文字ナルコトトヲ
知ラシム

五新文字ノ名稱ハ次ノ如シ

D＝dee　　　u＝ゆー

T＝tee　　　y＝わい

h＝āch

5.　五新字ノ名稱及ビ發音ト七新語ノ發音及ビ譯解
トノ練習ヲナサシメ次ニ本課四文章ノ讀方及ビ譯解ヲ
練習セシム

6. 書　方

Yes, I see the book on the desk.

此ノ文章ノ讀方及ビ譯解ヲナサシムベシ

讀方ハ

Yes,' I see the⌒book on the⌒desk`.

譯解ハ

然リ余ハ机ノ上ニ書物ヲ見ル

————————

(13)

第 五 課

I. 復習

A, B, D, I, P, T, Y.

a, b, d, e, g, h, i, k, n, o, p, s, t, u, y.

a̤, ănd, pĕn, bŏŏk, bĭg, ĭt, ĭṣ, yĕs, thē, ŏn, do̤, yo̤ṳ, seė, I.

Do⌢you see the⌢big desk′?

Yes′, I *see* the⌢big desk‵.

I see the⌢book and the⌢pen‵.

A pen and a book. It is a big book. Yes, I see the book on the desk.

2. て－ぶるノ實物又ハ圖畫ヲ 全級ノ生徒ニ示シテ 之ニ指サシナガラ

Is this a desk?

ト問ヒ首ヲ振リナガラ

No, it is not a desk.

ト答ヘ又

(14)

What is it?

It is a table.

ノ問答ヲナシ次ニ机トてーぶるトノ 區別ヲ示スタメニ
手眞似ヲ用ヒテ

That is a desk, but this is a table.

ト云フ。斯ノ如クスルコト數回ニ及ビ 生徒ヲシテ其ノ
大意ヲ悟ラシメ更ニ各文章ノ意義ヲ説明シテ 此ノ會話
ヲ繰返シ次ノ諸點ヲ教フ

(1) this, that ノ th ハ the ノ th ト同ジキコト

(2) nō ハのーニアラズシテのーうナルコト

(3) not ノ母音ハ on ノ ŏ ト同ジキコト

(4) what ハ hwŏt ノ如キ音ニシテ十分 練習ヲ要ス
ルコト

(5) table ノ tā ハてーニアラズシテてーいナルコト

(6) l ハ日本人ニ取リテ 最モ 困難ナル音ノ中ノ一ナ
レバ舌ノ位地其ノ他該音ノ發音ニ關スル心得ヲ 明カニ
説明シ正確ナル音ヲ示スコト

(7) but ノ ŭ ハ日本語ニナキ音ナレバ丁寧明瞭ニ之
ヲ説明スベキコト

(8) 母音ヲ伴ハザル子音ヲ 發音スル時 母音ヲ交ヘ
ザルコト

(9) 疑問文ノ末尾ハ音調ヲ高メ 非疑問文ノ末尾ハ

(15)

音調ヲ低クスベキハ既ニ教ヘシ所ナレド第三文ノ如ク
what ニテ始マル疑問文ハ矢張末尾ノ音調ヲ低クスベ
キコト

3. 成ルベク多數ノ生徒ヲシテ實物又ハ圖畫ニヨリ
本課五文章ノ發音及ビ譯解ヲ試ミシメ若シ誤謬アル時
ハ一々丁寧ニ之ヲ訂正ス

4. 次ニ此ノ五文章ヲ順次黒板ニ書キ反復其ノ讀方
及ビ譯解ヲ教ヘ發音ニ關シ次ノ三點ヲ說明ス

(1) wh ハ w ト同一ニアラズ hw ノ如キ音ナルコト

(2) what ノ a ハ ŏn 又ハ nŏt ノ ŏ ト同一ノ音ナル
コト

(3) table ノ e ハ發音セザルコト

讀方ハ

(1) Is this a⌒desk′?

(2) No′, it⌒is *not* a⌒desk‵.

(3) What *is*⌒it‵?

(4) It⌒is a⌒*table‵*.

(5) That is a⌒desk′, but this is a⌒table‵.

譯解ハ

(1) 是ハ(一脚ノ)机デアルカ

(2) 否ソレハ(一脚ノ)机デナイ

(3) ソレハ何デアルカ

（　16　）

(4)　ソレハ（一脚ノ）てーぶるデアル

(5)　アレハ（一脚ノ）机デアルガ是ハ（一脚ノ）てーぶ
るデアル

次ニ三箇ノ新文字ノ名稱及ビ發音ヲ示シ　N　ハ　n　ノ
頭文字ナルコトヲ知ラシム

　三新文字ノ名稱ハ次ノ如シ

　　　N＝ĕn　　　　l＝ĕl　　　　W＝dŭb'l-ɑ

5.　三新字ノ名稱及ビ發音ト七新語ノ發音及ビ譯解
トノ練習ヲナサシメ次ニ本課五文章ノ讀方及ビ譯解ヲ
練習セシム

6. 書方

No. That is not a desk, but a table.

此ノ文章ノ讀方及ビ譯解ヲナサシムベシ

讀方ハ

No'.　That⌒is not a⌒*desk'*, but a⌒*table'*.

譯解ハ

否ソレハ（一脚ノ）机デナクシテ（一脚ノ）てーぶるデ
アル

———

第 六 課

本課ハ第一課ヨリ第五課マデニ敎ヘタル所ヲ復習セ
シムルモノニシテ一字一語又ハ一音タリトモ未ダ記憶
シ得ザルモノアラバ決シテ次課ニ進ムベカラズ

1. 頭文字　九個

A, B, D, I, N, P, T, W, Y.

各字ノ名稱及ビ發音ヲ練習セシメ a, b, d, i, n, p, t, y
ノ頭文字ヲ問ヒ次ニ此ノ九箇ノ頭文字ノ書方ヲ練習セ
シム

2. 小文字　十六箇

a, b, d, e, g, h, i, k, l, n, o, p, s, t, u, y.

各字ノ名稱及ビ發音ヲ練習セシメ A, B, D, I, N, P,
T, Y ノ小文字ヲ問ヒ次ニ此ノ十六箇ノ小文字ノ書方
ヲ練習セシム

3. 母音　十二箇

á, ă, ĕ, ĭ, ŏ, ŭ, o͞o, o͝o, ā, ē, ĭ, ō.

是ハ文字ニヨラズシテ唯聲音ノミヲ敎フルノ目的ナ
レバ what ノ ạ ハ ŏ ノ中ニ入リ do̧ 及ビ yo̧u ノ ǫ ハ
o͞o ノ中ニ入ルナリ先ヅ此ノ十二箇ノ母音ノ練習ヲナ
シ各母音ヲ含メル單語ヲ舉ゲシム

4. 子音　十三箇

b, d, g, k, l, n, p, s, t, y, z, wh, th.

（ 18 ）

是モ文字ニアラズシテ唯聲音ノミヲ教フルノ目的ナ
レバ ş ヲ z ノ中ニ入レ wh, th ヲモ含ム。先ヅ此ノ十三
箇ノ子音ノ練習ヲナシ各子音ヲ含メル 單語ヲ擧ゲシム

5. 單語　二十二箇

各單語ノ發音及ビ譯解ヲ練習シ次ニ各 單語ヲ含メル
句又ハ文章ヲ擧ゲシム

6. 本課八文章ノ讀方及ビ譯解ヲ練習シ殊ニ音調ノ
接續及ビ抑揚ニ注意スベシ。 又成ルベク直譯ノ弊ヲ避
ケテ純良ナル日本文ニ譯スベシ

讀方ハ次ノ如クナルベシ

(1)　*What* is on the table?

(2)　A *pen* is on the table.

(3)　Is that a *book*?

(4)　Yes. That is a big *book*.

(5)　Do you see the desk?

(6)　Yes, I *see* the desk.

(7)　That is not a *table*, but a *desk*.

(8)　Is it not a big desk?

譯解ハ大凡次ノ如クナルベシ

(1)　何ガて－ぶるノ上ニアルカ

(2)　（一本ノ）ぺんガて－ぶるノ上ニアル

(19)

(3) ソレハ(一冊ノ)書物デアルカ

(4) 然リソレハ(一冊ノ)大ナル書物デアル

(5) 汝ハ机ヲ見ルカ

(6) 然リ余ハ机ヲ見ル

(7) ソレハ(一脚ノ)てーぶるデナクシテ(一脚ノ)机デアル

(8) ソレハ(一脚ノ)大ナル机デナイカ

7. 書 方

Do you see a book on the big table?

此ノ文章ノ讀方及ビ譯解ヲナサシムベシ

讀方ハ

Do⌒you see a⌒book on the⌒big table′?

譯解ハ

汝ハ大ナルてーぶるノ上ニ(一冊ノ)書物ヲ見ルカ

————

第 七 課

1. 復 習

(1) Do⌒you see the⌒book′?

(2) Yes′, I *see* the⌒book on the⌒desk‵.

(20)

(3)　Is this a⌒big table′?

(4)　No′, that⌒is *not* a⌒big·table‵.

(5)　What is⌒it‵?

(6)　Is⌒it a⌒pen′?

(7)　Yes′, it⌒*is* a⌒pen‵.

(8)　You see the⌒book and the⌒pen‵.

(9)　It⌒is not a⌒*table′*, but a⌒*desk‵*.

A book and a pen. Do you see the book? Yes, I see the book on the desk. No. That is not a desk, but a table.

2.　小サキ椅子ノ實物ヲ全級ノ生徒ニ示シテ之ニ指
サシラガラ

Here is a little chair.

ト云ヒ又小サキ腰掛ノ實物又ハ圖畵ヲ指サシナガラ

There is a little bench.

ト云ヒ次ニ

Can you see the chair?

ト問ヒ

(21)

Yes, I can see it.

ト答ヘ又手眞似ヲ以テ

You may sit down on it.

ト云ヒ御辭儀ヲナシナガラ

Thank you.

ト答フ。斯ノ如クスルコト數回ニ及ビ生徒ヲシテ其ノ大意ヲ悟ラシメ更ニ各文章ノ意義ヲ説明シテ此ノ會話ヲ繰返シ次ノ諸點ヲ敎フ

(1) Here ハひあニアラズシテひーあナルコト

(2) little ノ發音ハ頗ル困難ニシテ先ヅ l ノ音ヲ明確ニシ次ニりっとるト引掛ケズシテ唯 lﾟtl ト短ク發音スルコト

(3) châir 及 thêre ノ母音ハ全ク同一ナルコトヲ説キ其ノ音ヲ正確ニ示スコト

(4) chair 及 there ノ r ヲ發音スルニ必要ナル舌ノ位地ヲ説明スルコト

(5) bench ハべんちニアラズシテ べんch ナルコト

(6) sit ヲ shit ト誤マラザル樣注意スルコト

(7) thank ノ th ヲ明瞭ニ發音スルコト

3. 成ルベク多數ノ生徒ヲシテ實物又ハ圖書ニヨリ本課六文章ノ發音及ビ譯解ヲ試ミシメ若シ誤謬アル時ハ一々丁寧ニ之ヲ訂正ス

（ 22 ）

4. 次ニ此ノ六文章ヲ順次黒板ニ書キ反復其ノ讀方
及ビ譯解ヲ教ヘ次ノ諸點ヲ說明ス

（1） Here, little, there ノ最終ノ e ハ發音セザルコト

（2） little ノ前半 lit ヲ高調ニ讀ムコト

（3） down ハどーんニアラズシテだうんナルコト

（4） thank ノ th ハ the, this, that, there 等ノ th ト
異ナリ前者ハ清音ナレドモ後者ハ濁音ナルコト

（5） Here is 及ビ there is ヲ續ケテ讀ミひーありず
及ビぜーありずトナスコト

（6） Can you ヲ續ケテ讀ミきやに⌢ゆートナスコト
是ハ n ヲ發音スル時舌端ヲ上顎ニ附着スルニ由ルコト

（7） Thank you ヲ續ケテ讀ミさんき⌢ゆートナスコ
ト

讀方ハ

（1） Here⌢is a⌢little chair⸜.

（2） There⌢is a⌢little bench⸜.

（3） Can⌢you see the⌢chair′?

（4） Yes,′ I can see⌢it⸜.

（5） You may sit *down* on⌢it⸜.

（6） Thank⌢you⸜.

譯解ハ

（1） 玆ニ（一脚ノ）小サキ椅子ガアル

(23)

(2)　ソコニ(一脚ノ)小サキ腰掛ガアル

(3)　汝ハ椅子ヲ見ルコトガ出來ルカ

(4)　然リ余ハソレヲ見ルコトガ出來ル

(5)　汝ハソレニ坐シテモ宜シイ

(6)　有リ難ウ

次ニ六箇ノ新文字ノ名稱及ビ發音ヲ示シ H ハ h ノ頭文字ナルコト、w ハ W ノ小文字ナルコト及ビ C ト c ト ハ同文字ニシテ前者ハ頭文字後者ハ小文字ナルコトヲ知ラシム

六新文字ノ名稱ハ次ノ如シ

$$C = c = see \qquad r = är$$
$$H = āch \qquad w = dŭb'l\text{-}ū$$
$$m = ēm$$

5.　六新字ノ名稱及ビ發音ト十新語ノ發音及ビ譯解トノ練習ヲナサシメ次ニ本課六文章ノ讀方及ビ譯解ヲ練習セシム

6.　綴 字

是ハ啻ニ綴字ノ練習ノミナラズ發音ノ練習ニモ供センガ爲メナレバ先ヅ茲ニ揭グタル六語ノ發音ヲ聞キテ綴字ヲナサシムルコトト綴字ヲ示シテ發音ヲナサシムルコトト兩樣ノ練習ヲナスベシ

(24)

7. 書 方

Can you sit down on the chair?

此ノ文章ノ讀方及ビ譯解ヲナサシムベシ

讀方ハ

Can⌢you sit⌢down on the⌢chair′?

譯解ハ

汝ハ椅子ノ上ニ腰掛ケルコトガ出來ルカ

第 八 課

1. 復 習

A, B, C, D, H, I, N, P, T, W, Y.

a, b, c, d, e, g, h, i, k, l, m, n, o, p, r, s, t, u, w, y.

a̤, bŏok, bǐg, ǐ, yĕs, thē, ŏn, dọ, yọu, sēẹ, Ī, nō, whạt, tāblẹ, bŭt, hērẹ, châir, thêrẹ, bĕnch, căn, māy, down, thănk, lǐt′tlẹ.

Can⌢you see the⌢little bench′?

No′, I can *not* see⌢it′.

There⌢is a⌢big book on the⌢chair′.

(25)

What is there on the table ?

A *pen* is *on* it .

You may sit *down* on the chair .

Thank you .

ben, den, ken, pen, ten.

It is a big book. Yes, I see the book on the desk. No. That is not a desk, but a table. Do you see a book on the big table ? Can you sit down on the chair ?

2. 先ヅ生徒ノ鉛筆数本ヲ取リ全級ノ生徒ニ示シテ後是等鉛筆ノ持主ナル生徒ノ一人ニ向ヒ

Which is your pencil?

ト問ヒ其ノ生徒ニ代リテ其ノ鉛筆ヲ取リ

This is my pencil.

ト答ヘ又

Isn't this your pencil?

ト問ヒ

No, That is not my pencil.

(26)

ト答フ次ニ他ノ一人ノ生徒ニ代リテ

My pencil is in the bag.

ト云ヒ

Whose bag is it?

ト問フ。又或一人ノ生徒ニ向ヒ

Is it yours?

ト問ヒ又同人ニ代リテ

Yes, it is mine.

ト答フ。此ノ間恰好ノ手眞似等ヲ用ヒ之ヲ繰返スコト
數回ニ及ビ生徒ヲシテ其ノ大意ヲ悟ラシメ更ニ各文章
ノ意義ヲ説明シテ此ノ會話ヲ繰返シ次ノ諸點ヲ敎フ

　　(1)　whĭch ハ wĭch ニアラズシテ hwĭch ナルコト

　　(2)　your ハ よーあ ニアラズシテ ゆーあ ナルコト

　　(3)　pencil ハ ぺんしる (penshil) ニアラザルコト

　　(4)　mȳ ノ ȳ ハ ī ト同音ナルコト

　　(5)　isn't ハ いずんと ニアラズシテ い znt ナルコト

　　(6)　whose ハ hōōs ナルコト

　　(7)　băg, ノ母音ハ ănd ノ母音ト同ジキコト

　　(8)　whose 及ビ yours ヲ hōōz 及ビ yōorz ト敎フル
ハ大ニ我ガ邦ノ學生ヲ誤マルノ基ニシテ現今此ノ弊ヲ
蒙ムルモノ非常ニ多ク hōōzụ 及ビ yōorzụ ト發音スル
ヲ通常トス故ニ寧ロ hōōs 及ビ yōors ト敎フルヲ可ト

（ 27 ）

ス是レ本書ニ於テ特ニ此ノ種ノ s ヲ z ト發音セザル所
以ナリ

3. 成ルベク多數ノ生徒ヲシテ實物ニヨリ本課ノ文
章ノ發音及ビ譯解ヲ試ミシメ若シ誤謬アル時ハ一々丁
寧ニ之ヲ訂正ス

4. 次ニ此ノ八文章ヲ順次黑板ニ書キ反復其ノ讀方
及ビ譯解ヲ敎ヘ次ノ諸點ヲ說明ス

（1） pencil ノ前半 pen ヲ高調ニスルコト

（2） isn't ハ is not ヲ約メタルモノニテ apostrophe
（'）ハ省略ノ符號ナルコト

（3） whose 及ビ mine ノ最後ノ e ハ發音セザルコト

（4） which, pencil, bag, whose, yours ノ語尾ヲ ち,
る, ぐ, す, すトナスコトナク唯子音ノミトナスベキコ
ト

（5） whose ノ wh ハ hw ノ音ニアラズシテ單ニ h ノ
音ナルコト

（6） which is, this is, that is, the bag, is it, it is, 等ハ
急速ニ續ケテ讀ムコト
讀方ハ

（1） *Which* is your pencil?

（2） *This* is my pencil.

（3） Isn't *this* your pencil?

(28)

(4) No`.  That⌒is *not* my pencil`.

(5) *My* pencil is in the⌒bag`.

(6) *Whose* bag *is*⌒it`?

(7) Is⌒it *yours*'?

(8) Yes', it⌒*is* mine`.

譯解ハ

(1) ドレガ汝ノ鉛筆デアルカ

(2) 是ガ余ノ鉛筆デアル

(3) 是ハ汝ノ鉛筆デナイカ

(4) 否ソレハ余ノ鉛筆デナイ

(5) 余ノ鉛筆ハかばんノ中ニアル

(6) ソレハ誰ノかばんデアルカ

(7) ソレハ汝ノデアルカ

(8) 然リソレハ余ノデアル

次ニ新文字 M ノ名稱及ビ發音ヲ示シ是ハ m ノ頭文字ナルコトヲ知ラシム

　新字ノ名稱次ノ如シ

$$M = \breve{e}m$$

5.　一新字ノ名稱及ビ發音ト十新語ノ發音及ビ譯解トノ練習ヲナサシメ次ニ本課八文章ノ 讀方及ビ譯解ヲ練習セシム

(29)

6. 綴 字

it, bit, pit, sit, tit, chit.

先ヅ此ノ六語ノ發音ヲ聞キテ綴字ヲナサシメ 次ニ綴
字ヲ示シテ發音ヲナサシムベシ

7. 書 方

My pencil is not in the bag.

此ノ文章ノ讀方及ビ譯解ヲナサシムベシ

讀方ハ

My⌒pencil is not in the⌒bag`.

譯解ハ

余ノ鉛筆ハかばんノ中ニナイ

第 九 課

1. 復 習

A, B, C, D, H, I, M, N, P, T, W, Y.

a, b, c, d, e, g, h, i, k, l, m, n, o, p, r, s, t,
u, w, y.

à, bŏok, ĭṣ, thē, ŏn, dọ, yọừrs, sēệ, mȳ, nō, whạt,
tāblệ, bŭt, hērệ, mīnệ, châir, thêrệ, pĕn'çĭl, bĕnch,
căn, māẏ, băg, down, thănk, ĭṣn't, lĭt'tlệ.

(30)

Which is your bag`?

My bag is on the chair`.

Isn't that *your* pencil'?

Yes', that *is* mine`.

Whose book is this`?

It is not *my* book`.

ben, ken, ten, bit, sit, chit.

Yes, I see the book on the desk`

No. That is not a table, but a

desk. Do you see a book on the big

table? Can you sit down on the

chair? My pencil is not in the

bag.

2. 机ノ上ニいんき壺ヲ置キタル有樣ヲ實物又ハ圖
畫ニヨリテ全級ノ生徒ニ示シナガラ

What is on the desk?

ト問ヒいんき壺ヲ指サシナガラ

An inkstand is on the desk.

(31)

ト答ヘ又

What do you find in the inkstand?

ト問ヒ

I find some ink in it.

ト答ヘ次ニ其ノいんきヲ指サシナガラ

Is that ink black or red?

ト問ヒ

It is black.

ト答フ

Is it not red ink?

ト反問シ首ヲ振リナガラ

No, it is not red ink.

ト答フ。斯ノ如クスルコト數回ニ及ビ生徒ヲシテ其ノ大意ヲ悟ラシメ更ニ各文章ノ意義ヲ説明シテ此ノ會話ヲ繰返シ次ノ諸點ヲ教フ

(1)　ăn, blăck ノ ă ハ ănd 又ハ căn ノ ă ト同一ナルコト

(2)　an inkstand, in it ヲ接續スル時ハ n ト i ト結合シテにトナルコト

(3)　f ノ音ヲ出スニ必要ナル唇ノ位地ヲ明示スルコト

(32)

(4)　find ノ母音ハ $\bar{1}$, $m\bar{y}$ ノ母音ト同ジキコト

(5)　sȯme ノ母音ハ bŭt ノ母音ト同ジキモノニテさむニアラザルコト

(6)　ôr ハ ạr ニシテ ōr ニアラザルコト又 r ハ chair, there ノ r ノ如キコト

(7)　red ノ r ヲ發音スルニ必要ナル舌ノ位置ヲ說明スルコト

(8)　inkstand, find, red ノ語尾ハ ど ニアラズ ink, black ノ語尾ハ く 又ハ き ニアラズ唯 d 又ハ k ノ子音ノミナルコト

3.　成ルベク多數ノ生徒ヲシテ實物又ハ圖畫ニヨリ本課八文章ノ發音及ビ譯解ヲ試ミシメ若シ誤謬アル時ハ一々丁寧ニ之ヲ訂正ス

4.　次ニ此ノ八文章ヲ順次黑板ニ書キ反復其ノ讀方及ビ譯解ヲ敎ヘ次ノ諸點ヲ說明ス

(1)　inkstand ノ前半 ink ヲ高調ニスルコト

(2)　some ハ そー m ニアラズシテ sŭm ナルコト又其ノ最後ノ e ハ發音セザルコト

(3)　what is, the desk, an inkstand, do you, the inkstand, in it, it is, is it, red ink 等ハ急速ニ續ケテ讀ムコト

(4)　ăn ハ ạ ト同意義ナルモ前者ハ母音ノ前ニ用ヒ

（ 33 ）

後者ハ子音ノ前ニ用フルコト

讀方ハ

(1) What⌢is on the⌢desk`?

(2) An⌢*inkstand* is on the⌢desk`.

(3) What do⌢you find in the⌢inkstand`?

(4) I find some *ink* in⌢it`.

(5) Is that ink black´ or red`?

(6) It⌢is black`.

(7) Is⌢it not red⌢ink´?

(8) No´, it⌢is *not* red⌢ink`.

譯解ハ

(1) 何ガ机ノ上ニアルカ

(2) （一ノ）いんき壺ガ机ノ上ニアル

(3) 汝ハいんき壺ノ中ニ何ヲ認ムルカ

(4) 余ハソノ中ニ多少ノいんきヲ認ム

(5) ソノいんきハ黒色カ赤色カ

(6) ソレハ黒色デアル

(7) ソレハ赤いんきデナイカ

(8) 否ソレハ赤いんきデナイ

次ニ新文字 f ノ名稱及ビ發音ヲ示ス。新字ノ名稱次ノ如シ

(34)

f＝ĕf

5. 一新字ノ名稱及ビ發音ト八新語ノ發音及ビ譯解
トノ練習ヲナサシメ次ニ本課八文章ノ讀方及ビ譯解ヲ
練習セシム

6. 綴字

bo, go, ho, lo, no, so.

先ヅ此ノ五語ノ發音ヲ問キテ綴字ヲナサシメ次ニ綴
字ヲ示シテ發音ヲナサシムベシ

7. 書方

What do you find in the ink-stand? I find some black ink in it.

是等ノ文章ノ讀方及ビ譯解ヲナサシムベシ
讀方ハ

What do⌢you find in the⌢inkstand`?　I find
some black *ink* in⌢it.

譯解ハ

汝ハいんき壺ノ中ニ何ヲ認ムルカ、余ハ其ノ中ニ多
少ノ黒いんきヲ認ム

(35)

第 十 課

I. 復習

A, B, C, D, H, I, M, N, P, T, W, Y.

a, b, c, d, e, f, g, h, i, k, l, m, n, o, p, r, s, t, u, w, y.

à, bŏŏk, bĭg, thē, ŏn, dọ, yọ̀ụrs, sēḝ, mȳ, nō, whạt, tāblḝ, bŭt, hērḝ, find, ĭnk, châîr, thêrḝ, rĕd, bĕnch, căn, māȳ, blăck, down, thănk, ĭṣn't, sȯmḝ, ôr, ĭnk′stănd, pĕn′çĭl.

What⌒is in your bag`?

A⌒*pencil* is in my bag`.

Do⌒you find an⌒inkstand on the⌒desk′?

No,′ I do *not* find⌒it`.

Is⌒your pencil black′?

My pencil is *not black*′, but *red.*`

ben, pen, men, it, pit, tit, go, lo, so.

No. That is not a table, but a desk. Do you see a book on the

(36)

big table?   Can you sit down on the chair?   My pencil is not in the bag.   What do you find in the inkstand?

2.　きゃっぷ及ビはっとノ實物又ハ圖畫ヲ全級ノ生徒ニ示シナガラ手眞似ヲ用ヒテ

Have you a cap?

ト問ヒ

Yes, I have a cap.

ト答ヘ次ニはっとヲ指サシテ

Is this a cap too?

ト問ヒ首ヲ振リナガラ

No, it is not a cap, but a hat.

ト答フ又一ノきゃっぷヲ指サシテ

Is this John's cap?

ト問ヒ

O, no!   It is Roy's cap.

ト答ヘ而シテ後

His cap is just like mine.

ト云ヒタル時點頭キナガラ

You are quite right.

ト云フ。斯ノ如クスルコト數回ニ及ビ生徒ヲシテ其ノ大意ヲ悟ラシメ更ニ各文章ノ意義ヲ説明シテ此ノ會話ヲ繰返シ次ノ諸點ヲ敎フ

(1) have ノ v ハ f ノ濁音ト云フベキモノニシテ日本語ニハ存セザル音ナレバ之ヲ明示スルコト

(2) too ヲつート區別スルコト

(3) Roy's ハろーいすニアラズろーういすニモアラズろいすナルコト

(4) jŭst ノ母音ハ bŭt ノ母音ト同ジキコト

(5) quīte ノ quī ヲ正確ニ發音スルコト

3. 成ルベク多數ノ生徒ヲシテ實物又ハ圖畫ニヨリ本課ハ文章ノ發音及ビ譯解ヲ試ミシメ若シ誤謬アル時ハ一々丁寧ニ之ヲ訂正ス

4. 次ニ此ハ文章ヲ順次黑板ニ書キ反復其ノ讀方及ビ譯解ヲ敎ヘ次ノ諸點ヲ説明ス

(1) have, like, are, quite ノ最後ノ e ハ發音セザルコト

(2) like ヲらいく又ハらいきト云ハズシテ最後ハ唯子音ノミニテ止ムルコト have, cap, hat, John's, Roy's, his, just, quite, right ノ如ク子音ニテ終ル語ハ皆此ノ注

(38)

意ヲ要ス

(3)　oo ハ ウ ー ナルコト

(4)　John's, Roy's ノ終ノ ('s) ハ『何某の』ト云フ時ニ用フル形ニシテ發音ハ矢張 z トナサズシテ s トナスベキコト

(5)　his ノ s ハ濁音トナシ hĭz ト讀ムベキコト

(6)　quīte ノ quī ヲかいト讀マズ又回, 會, 快, 等ノ くゎいト同一ニモ讀マズ少シク緩ク讀ミテ くゎいトナスコト

(7)　right, ノ gh ハ全ク無音ナルコト

(8)　Have you, a cap, it is, a hat, John's cap, His cap, you are, quite right 等ハ急速ニ續ケテ讀ムコト

(9)　is ト are トハ同意義ナルモ各其ノ用ヒラルヽ場合ノ異ナルヲ注意記憶スベキコト

(10)　John, Roy　ノ如キ人名ノ最初ハ頭文字ヲ用フルコト

(11)　感嘆文ノ最後ニハ Exclamation mark (!) ヲ附スルコト

讀方ハ

(1)　Have⌒you a⌒cap′?

(2)　Yes′, I *have* a⌒cap`.

(3)　Is *this* a⌒cap′ too′?

(39)

(4) No', it⌒is *not* a cap', but a⌒*hat*`.

(5) Is this John's⌒cap'?

(6) O, *no*! It⌒is *Roy's*⌒cap`.

(7) His⌒cap is just like mine`.

(8) You⌒are quite⌒right`.

譯解ハ

(1) 汝ハ(一ノ)きゃっぷヲ有ツカ

(2) 然リ余ハ(一ノ)きゃっぷヲ有ツ

(3) 是モ亦(一ノ)きゃっぷデアルカ

(4) 否ソレハきゃっぷデナクシテ(一ノ)はっとデアル

(5) 是ハじょんノきゃっぷデアルカ

(6) イーヤ, ソレハろいノきゃっぷデアル

(7) 彼ノきゃっぷハ丁度余ノ(きゃっぷ)ノ樣デアル

(8) 汝ノ云フ通リデアル

次ニ六新文字ノ名稱及ビ發音ヲ示シ J ト j トハ同一
ノ文字ニシテ前者ハ頭文字後者ハ小文字ナルコト又 O,
R ハ o, r ノ頭文字ナルコトヲ知ラシム

六新字ノ名稱ハ次ノ如シ

J＝j＝jā   v＝vee

O＝を－う   q＝きゅー

R＝är

5. 六新字ノ名稱及ビ發音ト十三新語ノ發音及ビ譯
解トノ練習ヲナサシメ次ニ本課八文章ノ 讀方及ビ譯解
ヲ練習セシム

6. 綴字

bat, cat, fat, hat, mat, pat, rat, sat.

先ヅ此ノ八語ノ發音ヲ聞キテ 綴字ヲナサシメ次ニ綴
字ヲ示シテ發音ヲナサシムベシ

7. 書方

Have you Roy's cap?   O, no!
I have John's cap.   It is just like
mine.

是等ノ文章ノ讀方及ビ譯解ヲナサシムベシ

讀方ハ

Have⌢you Roy's⌢cap´?   O´, no`!   I have
John's⌢cap`.  It⌢is just like *mine`*.

譯解ハ

汝ハろいノきゃっぷヲ有ツカ、 イーヤ、余ハじょんノ
きゃっぷヲ有ッ、 ソレハ丁度余ノ(きゃっぷ)ノ樣デア
ル、

————————

(41)

第 十 一 課

1. 復習

A, B, C, D, H, I, J, M, N, O, P, R, T, W, Y.

a, b, c, d, e, f, g, h, i, j, k, l, m, n, o, p, q, r, s, t, u, v, w, y.

à, bŏŏk, bĭg, thē, Jŏhn's, dọ, yọụrs, sēẹ, mȳ, nō, whạt, tāblẹ, jŭst, hērẹ, fĭnd, quĭtẹ, hĭṣ, châir, thêrẹ, rĕd, bĕnch, hăvẹ, căn, māȳ, down, thănk, ĭṣn't, sọmẹ, ôr, tōō, Roy's, ärẹ, rĭght, pĕn'çĭl.

Have⌒you an⌒inkstand'?

No', I have not an⌒inkstand⸜.

Is⌒it Roy's pencil'?

Yes', it⌒*is* his pencil⸜.

Your hat is just like *mine*⸜.

You may sit⌒*down* on this chair⸜.

ten, den, bit, wit, ho, no, fat, rat.

Do you see a book on the big table? Can you sit down on the

(42)

chair? My pencil is not in the bag. What do you find in the ink-stand? John's cap is just Roy's cap.

2. 箱及ビ小刀ノ實物又ハ圖畫ヲ全級ノ生徒ニ示シタル後物ヲ探スガ如キ身振ヲナシナガラ

Where is your penknife?

ト問ヒ手眞似ヲ以テ箱ニ指サシナガラ

My penknife must be in that box.

ト答ヘ其ノ箱ヲ檢査シテ

No, it is not in this box.

ト云フ。依ツテ手眞似ヲ以テ

Please show me the box.

ト云フ。次ニ一ノ小刀ニ指サシテ

Whose penknife is this?

ト問ヒ

It is Frank's.

ト答ヘ又

This must be a new penknife.

（ 43 ）

ト云ヘバ首ヲ振リナガラ

No, it is an old penknife.

ト答フ。斯ノ如クスルコト數回ニ及ビ生徒ヲシテ其ノ
大意ヲ悟ラシメ更ニ各文章ノ意義ヲ説明シテ此ノ會話
ヲ繰返シ次ノ諸點ヲ敎フ

(1) whêre ノ wh ハ what, which ノ wh ノ如ク ê ハ
châir, thêre ノ母音ノ如キコト

(2) please ノ始 p ト l トノ間ニ母音ヲ插入セザルコ
ト

(3) new ヌーニアラズシテにゅーナルコト

(4) ōld ノ ō ハ をーニアラズシテ をーうナルコト又
l ト d トノ間ニ母音ヲ插入セザルコト

(5) an old ヲ接續シテ n ト o ト ヲ結合シ『の』ノ音
ヲ生ズルコト

(6) penknife, must, box, please, Frank's, old ノ語尾
ヲ ふ、すと、くす、ず、くす、ど トナサズシテ子音ノミ
ニ止ムルコト又 Frank's ノ F ト r トノ間ニ母音ヲ插入
セザルコト

(7) shōw ハ しょーう ニシテ しょーー ナラザルコト

3. 成ルベク多數ノ生徒ヲシテ實物又ハ圖畫ニヨリ
本課ハ文章ノ發音及ビ譯解ヲ試ミシメ若シ誤謬アル時
ハー々丁寧ニ之ヲ訂正ス

(44)

4. 次ニ此ノ八文章ヲ順次 黒板ニ書キ反復其ノ讀方及ビ譯解ヲ敎ヘ次ノ諸點ヲ說明ス

（1） where, penknife, please, ノ最後ノ e ハ發音セザルコト

（2） penknife ノ前半 pen ヲ高調ニスルコト又 k ハ發音セザルコト

（3） box ノ x ハ ks ト均シキコト

（4） please ノ s ハ濁音ニシテ z ナルコト

（5） where is, must be, that box, it is, this box, show me, the box, whose penknife, is this, it is, a new, an old 等ハ急速ニ續ケテ讀ムコト

（6） Frank ハ人名ナルガ故ニ頭文字ヲ用ユルコト

（7） Please ハ「どーぞ」ト譯スベキ語ニテ丁寧ニ願意ヲ述ブル時用ヒラルルコト

讀方ハ

（1） Where⌒is your penknife`?

（2） My penknife must⌒be in that⌒box`.

（3） No,'it⌒is *not* in this⌒box`.

（4） Please *show*⌒me the⌒box`.

（5） *Whose* penknife is⌒this`?

（6） It⌒is *Frank's*`.

(45)

(7) This must⌒be a⌒new penknife`.

(8) No,′ it⌒is an⌒old penknife`.

譯解ハ

(1) 汝ノ小刀ハ何處ニアルカ

(2) 余ノ小刀ハ彼ノ箱ノ中ニアル筈デアル

(3) 否此ノ箱ノ中ニナイ

(4) ドーゾ箱ヲ私ニ見セテ下サイ

(5) 是ハ誰ノ小刀カ

(6) ソレハふらんくノデアル

(7) 是ハ(一挺ノ)新シキ小刀ニ相違ナイ

(8) 否ソレハ(一挺ノ)古キ小刀デアル

次ニ二新文字ノ名稱及ビ發音ヲ示シ F ハ f ノ頭文字ナルコトヲ教フ

二新文字ノ名稱ハ次ノ如シ

F＝ĕf　　　　　x＝ĕx

5. 二新字ノ名稱及ビ發音ト十新語ノ發音及ビ譯解トノ練習ヲナサシメ次ニ本課ハ文章ノ讀方及ビ譯解ヲ練習セシム

6. 綴 字

book, cook, hook, look, nook, rook, took.

先ヅ此ノ七語ノ發音ヲ聞キテ綴字ヲナサシメ次ニ綴字ヲ示シテ發音ヲナサシムベシ

(46)

7. 書方

Frank's penknife must be in that box. You are quite right.

是等ノ文章ノ讀方及ビ譯解ヲナサシムベシ

讀方ハ

Frank's penknife must⌒be in that⌒box.ˋ You⌒
are quite⌒right.ˋ

譯解ハ

ふらんくノ小刀ハ彼ノ箱ノ中ニアル筈デアル、汝ノ
言フ通リデアル、

第 十 二 課

本課ハ第一課ヨリ第十一課マデニ敎ヘタル所ヲ練習
セシムルモノニシテ一字一語又一音タリトモ未ダ記憶
シ得ザルモノアラバ決シテ次課ニ進ムベカラズ

1. 頭文字 十六箇

A, B, C, D, F, H, I, J, M, N, O, P, R, T, W, Y.

各字ノ名稱及ビ發音ヲ練習セシメ a, b, c, d, f, h, i, j,

（ 47 ）

m, n, o, p, r, t, w, y, ノ頭文字ヲ問ヒ次ニ此ノ十六箇ノ
頭文字ノ書方ヲ練習セシム

2. 小文字　二十五箇

a, b, c, d, e, f, g, h, i, j, k, l, m, n, o, p, q,
r, s, t, u, v, w, x, y.

各字ノ名稱及ビ發音ヲ練習セシメ A, B, C, D, F, H,
I, J, M, N, O, P, R, T, W, Y　ノ小文字ヲ問ヒ次ニ此ノ
二十五箇ノ小文字ノ書方ヲ練習セシム

3. 母音　十八箇

是ハ文字ニヨラズシテ唯聲音ノミヲ敎フルノ目的ナ
レバ ôr ノ ô ハ a̤ ノ中ニ入リ whạt ノ ạ ハ ŏ ノ中ニ入
リ sòme ノ ò ハ ŭ ノ中ニ入リ dọ 及 yo̤u ノ ọ ハ o͞o ノ
中ニ入リ thêre 及ビ whêre ノ ê ハ â ノ中ニ入リ new ノ
ew ハ ū ノ中ニ入リ Roy's ノ oy ハ oi ノ中ニ入リ
down ノ ow ハ ou ノ中ニ入ルナリ。　先ヅ此ノ十八箇
ノ母音ノ練習ヲナシ各母音ヲ含メル單語ヲ擧ゲシム

4. 子音　二十四箇

是モ文字ヲ敎フルニアラズシテ唯聲音ノミヲ敎フル
ノ目的ナレバ c̆ăn ノ c̆ ハ k ノ中ニ入リ ş ハ z ノ中ニ
入リ r (initial) ト r (final) トヲ區別シ th ト th̶ トヲ區別
シ qu, wh, th, ch 等ヲ含ム。　先ヅ此ノ二十四箇ノ子
音ノ練習ヲナシ各子音ヲ含メル單語ヲ擧ゲシム

(48)

5. 單語 七十三箇

各單語ノ發音及ビ譯解ヲ練習シ次ニ各單語ヲ合メル
句又ハ文章ヲ舉グシム

6. 本課十一文章ノ讀方及ビ譯解ヲ練習シ殊ニ音調
ノ接續及ビ抑場ニ注意スベシ又成ルベク直譯ノ弊ヲ避
ケテ純良ナル日本文ニ譯スベシ

讀方ハ

(1) Isn't this a⌒new hat'?

(2) That⌒is an⌒*old* hat.`

(3) Where⌒is your pencil`?

(4) My⌒pencil must⌒be in the⌒bag.`

(5) Have⌒you an⌒inkstand'?

(6) No', I have *not.*`

(7) Whose chair *is*⌒it`?

(8) Is⌒it yours'?

(9) No', it⌒is not *mine,'* but *Roy's.*`

(10) Isn't⌒it just like *John's'*?

(11) Yes', it⌒*is*`; You⌒are *right.*`

Semicolon (;) ハ文章ノ中間ニテ略゛意義ノ完結シタ
ル所ニ用ヒラルハ符號ナリ

譯解ハ

(49)

(1) 是ハ（一ノ）新シキはっとデナイカ

(2) ソレハ（一ノ）古キはっとデアル

(3) 汝ノ鉛筆ハ何處ニアルカ

(4) 余ノ鉛筆ハかばんノ中ニアル筈デアル

(5) 汝ハ（一ノ）いんき壺ヲ有ツカ

(6) 否余ハ有タヌ

(7) ソレハ誰ノ椅子デアルカ

(8) ソレハ汝ノデアルカ

(9) 否ソレハ余ノデハナクろいノデアル

(10) ソレハ丁度じょんノ（椅子）ノ樣デナイカ

(11) 然リソーデアル、汝ノ言フ通リデアル

7. 綴 字

cot, dot, got, hot, jot, lot, not, pot, rot, sot.

old, bold, cold, fold, gold, hold, mold, sold, told.

先ヅ是等ノ單語ノ發音ヲ聞キテ綴字ヲナサシメ次ニ
綴字ヲ示シテ發音ヲナサシムベシ

8. 書 方

*Where is your new hat?　It is
not here.　Have you a pencil?　Yes,
I have it.*

(50)

是等ノ文章ノ讀方及ビ譯解ヲナサシムベシ

讀方ハ

Where⌢is your new⌢hat`? It⌢is not *here*`.
Have⌢you a⌢pencil`? Yes´, I *have*⌢it`.

譯解ハ

汝ノ新シキ はっと ハ 何處ニアルカ、此處ニハ ナイ、
汝ハ （一ノ） 鉛筆ヲ有ツカ、然リ余ハ之ヲ有ツ、

第 十 三 課

1. 復習

(1) Isn't⌢this your pencil´?

(2) No´, that⌢is *not* my⌢pencil´, but *Frank's*`.

(3) Where⌢is my little book`?

(4) *Here*⌢is your little book`。

(5) Whose⌢cap *is*⌢it`?

(6) It must⌢be *John's*⌢cap`.

(7) Please show⌢me your penknife`.

(8) Have⌢you an⌢inkstand´?

(9) Yes´, I⌢*have*`.

(51)

(10)　What do⌢you find on the⌢desk`?

(11)　I find a⌢*book* and a⌢*pen* on the⌢desk`.

(12)　Which⌢is your⌢bag`?

(13)　Your⌢bag is just like *mine*`.

(14)　You⌢are quite⌢*right*`.

pen, hen, fit, lit, go, so, mat, rat, cook, nook, dot, jot, bold, told.

My pencil is not in the bag. What do you find in the inkstand? John's cap is just like Roy's cap. Frank's penknife must be in that box.　Have you a pencil?

2.　教師自カラ書物ヲ手ニ取リ上ゲナガラ

Take up your book.

ト云ヒ生徒ヲシテ之ニ倣ハシメ 又其ノ書物ヲ机上ニ置キナガラ

Put your book on the desk.

ト云ヒ又生徒ヲシテ之ニ倣ハシム。次ニ教師其ノ書物ヲ開キナガラ

(52)

Open the book.

ト云ヒ生徒ヲシテ其ノ書物ヲ開カシメ 又敎師其ノ書物ヲ閉デナガラ

Shut it.

ト云ヒ生徒ヲシテ之ニ倣ハシム。 次ニ手眞似ヲ用ヒテ

Can you read the book?

ト問ヒ點頭キナガラ

Yes, I can.

ト答ヘ乃チ手眞似ヲ用ヒテ

Very good.

ト云フ。 最後ニ

What is this book?

ト問ヒ

This is the First English Reader.

ト答ヘ直ニ點頭キナガラ

Quite right.

ト云フ。 斯ノ如クスルコト數回ニ及ビ生徒ヲシテ其ノ大意ヲ悟ラシメ更ニ各文章ノ意義ヲ說明シテ 此ノ會話ヲ繰返シ次ノ諸點ヲ敎フ

(1) ŭp 及ビ shŭt ノ母音ハ jŭst, mŭst ノ ŭ 及ビ sòme ノ ò ト同音ナルコト

(53)

(2) put ノ母音及ビ good ノ ŏŏ ハ book ノ ŏŏ ト同音ナルコト

(3) open ハ おっぷん ニアラズ おーぷん ニモアラズ おーうぷん ナルコト

(4) very ハ べり 又ハ べりー ニアラズ最初ノ子音ハ v ニシテ最後ノ母音ハ ĭ ナルコト

(5) first ノ ĭr 及ビ readĕr ノ ĕr ハ日本人ニ取リテ極メテ困難ナルモノナレバ之ヲ丁寧明瞭ニ教フルコト

(6) English ヲ えんぐりっし, えんぐりっしゅ, いんぎりっし, いんぎりっしゅ ナドト發音スルハ皆誤謬ニシテ最初ノ母音ヲ いト シ g 及ビ sh ノ後ニ母音ヲ加ヘズ ng ヲ鼻音トシ又 l ヲ正確ニ發音スベキコト

(7) take, up, put, shut, read, good, first 等ノ最後ニ母音ヲ加ヘザルコト

3. 成ルベク多數ノ生徒ヲシテ自カラ手眞似又ハ身振ヲナシナガラ本課十文章ノ發音及ビ譯解ヲ試ミシメ若シ誤謬アル時ハ一々丁寧ニ之ヲ訂正ス

4. 次ニ此ノ十文章ヲ順次黒板ニ書キ反復其ノ讀方及ビ譯解ヲ教ヘ次ノ諸點ヲ説明ス

(1) take ノ e ハ發音セザルコト

(2) put ハ pŭt ト讀マズ pŏŏt ト讀ムコト

(3) open ノ e ハ發音セザルコト又 ō ヲ高調ニスル

コト

(4) read ノ a ハ發音セザルコト

(5) very ヲ věry ト讀マズシテ věr'ў ト讀ミ其ノ前半 věr ヲ高調ニスルコト

(6) good ハ gōod ニアラズシテ gŏod ナルコト

(7) first ハ ふぁーすと ニアラズ ふぁるすと ニモアラズ fĕrst ナルコト

(8) Eng'lish ノ前半ヲ高調ニスルコト

(9) read'er ノ前半 rēad ヲ高調ニスルコト

(10) take up, the desk, the book, shut it, can you, I can, very good, what is, this book, this is, the First, quite right 等ハ急速ニ續ケテ讀ムコト

(11) First English Reader ハ特別ノ物名ナルガ故ニ頭文字ヲ用フルコト

讀方ハ

(1) Take⌒*up* your book`.

(2) Put your book on the⌒desk`.

(3) Open the⌒book`.

(4) *Shut*⌒it`.

(5) Can⌒you read the⌒book'?

(6) Yes', I⌒*can*`.

(55)

(7) Very⌒*good*`.

(8) What⌒is this⌒book`?

(9) This⌒is the⌒First English Reader`.

(10) Quite⌒right`.

譯解ハ

(1) 汝ノ書物ヲ取リ上ゲヨ

(2) 机ノ上ニ汝ノ書物ヲ置ケ

(3) 書物ヲ開ケ

(4) 閉ヂヨ

(5) 汝ハ書物ヲ讀ムコトガ出來ルカ

(6) 然リ余ハ出來ル

(7) 至極結構

(8) 此ノ書物ハ何デアルカ

(9) 是ハ第一英語讀本デアル

(10) 確カニ其ノ通リ

次ニ四新文字ノ名稱及ビ發音ヲ示シ S, V, E, Q ハ s, v, e, q ノ頭文字ナルコトヲ敎フ

四新文字ノ名稱ハ次ノ如シ

E＝いー　　　S＝ĕs

Q＝きゅー　　V＝vee

5. 四新字ノ名稱及ビ發音ト十一新語ノ發音及ビ譯

解トノ練習ヲナサシメ次ニ本課十文章ノ讀方及ビ譯解
ヲ練習セシム

6. 綴字

but, cut, gut, hut, nut, rut.

big, dig, fig, gig, pig, rig.

先ヅ是等ノ單語ノ發音ヲ聞キテ綴字ヲナサシメ次ニ
綴字ヲ示シテ發音ヲナサシムベシ

7. 書方

*Open your book. Shut it. This
is the First English Reader. Quite
right. Very good.*

是等ノ文章ノ讀方及ビ譯解ヲナサシムベシ

讀方ハ

Open your book˅. *Shut⌒it˅.* This⌒is the⌒
First English Reader˅. Quite⌒right˅. Very⌒
good˅.

譯解ハ

汝ノ書物ヲ開ケ、閉ヂヨ、是ハ第一英語讀本デアル
確ニ其ノ通リ、至極結構

(57)

第 十 四 課

I. 復習

A, B, C, D, E, F, H, I, J, M, N, O, P, Q, R, S, T, V, W, Y.

a, b, c, d, e, f, g, h, i, j, k, l, m, n, o, p, q, r, s, t, u, v, w, x, y.

a̤, go̽od, bĭg, thē, bŏx, do̤, yo̤ṳrs, sēe̤, mȳ, ō′pe̤n, wha̤t, tāke̤, jŭst, shŭt, rēa̤d′ēr, quīte̤, hĭs̤, châi̤r, whêre̤, rĕd, bĕnch, hă̆ve̤, ca̤n, māy̤, down, thănk, ĭs̤n′t, sóme̤, ôr, tō̤o. Roy′s, äre̤, rĭg̲ht, shōw̤, new, pṳt, vĕr′y̆, fĭrst, Eng′lĭsh, pen′k̲nīfe̤.

Take⌢*up* your pencil`.

Put⌢your bag on the⌢table`.

You *open* the⌢book′ and I *shut*⌢it`.

Is this the⌢First English Reader′?

Yes′, you⌢are quite⌢right`.

Please show⌢me your penknife`.

pen, hen, fit, lit, go, so, mat, rat, cook, nook, cut, hut, dig, pig.

What do you find in the ink-stand? John's cap is just like Roy's cap. Frank's penknife must be in that box. Have you a pencil? Open the First English Reader. Shut it. Quite right. Very good.

2. 圖畫ニヨリ鐵砲ヲ持テル男兒ト人形ヲ持テル女兒トヲ示シ先ヅ其ノ男兒ノ想像的會話ヲナシ

Are you a boy?

ト問ヒ男兒ニ代リテ

Yes, I am a boy.

ト答ヘ次ニ女兒ニ向ヒ

Are you also a boy?

ト問ヒ其女兒ニ代リテ

No, I am not a boy.

ト答ヘ引續キテ

I am a girl.

ト云フ次ニ男兒ヲ指シ且手眞似ヲ用ヒテ

(59)

The boy has a gun.

He is very proud of the gun.

ト云ヒ又女兒ヲ指シ且手眞似ヲ用ヒテ

The girl has a doll.

She is very fond of the doll.

ト云フ。斯ノ如クスルコト數回ニ及ビ生徒ヲシテ其ノ
大意ヲ悟ラシメ更ニ各文章ノ意義ヲ說明シテ此會話ヲ
繰返シ次ノ諸點ヲ敎フ

(1)　boy ハぼーいニアラズぼぅいニモアラズぼいナ
ルコト

(2)　al′sŏ ノ ạ ハ ôr ノ ô ト同音ナルコト又 ō ハ nō,
shōw, ōld 等ノ ō ト同音ナレドモ時間ノ短キコト

(3)　gǐrl ノ ǐr ハ fǐrst ノ ǐr ト同音ナルコト

(4)　gŭn ノ ŭ ハ bŭt, ŭp ノ ŭ ト同音ナルコト

(5)　proud ノ ou ハ down ノ ow ト同音ナルコト

(6)　ŏf, dŏll 及ビ fŏnd ノ ŏ ハ ŏn, nŏt, bŏx ノ ŏ ト同
音ナルコト

(7)　ăm 及ビ hăṣ ノ ă ハ băg, blăck, căn, hăt, ăn,
ănd, hăve, thănk, thăt 等ノ ă ト同音ナルコト

(8)　hē 及ビ shē ノ ē ハ bē, sēẹ ノ ē ト同音ナルコト

(9)　子音ヲ以ヲ終ル處ニ母音ヲ附加セザルコト

3. 成ルベク多數ノ生徒ヲシテ圖畵ニヨリ本課九文

（ 60 ）

章ノ發音及ビ譯解ヲ試ミシメ若シ誤謬アル時ハ一々丁寧ニ之ヲ訂正ス

4. 次ニ此ノ九文章ヲ順次黑板ニ書キ反復其ノ讀方及ビ譯解ヲ教ヘ次ノ諸點ヲ說明ス

（1） al'sŏ ノ前半 al ヲ高調ニスルコト

（2） gīrl ヲがーる又ハごーるトナサヾル樣注意スルコト

（3） hăṣ ノ語尾ハ s ノ淸音ニアラズシテ濁音ナルコト

（4） gŭn ヲぐん又ハがんトナサザルコト、ŭ ハ日本語ニナキ音ナレバ之ヲ明示スルコト

（5） proud ヲぷろーどト發音セザル樣注意スルコト

（6） of ノ f ハ v ト同一ノ音ヲ有スルコト

（7） dŏll ハどーるニアラザルコト

（8） are you, a boy, I am, a girl, the boy, a gun, he is, very proud, the gun, the girl, a doll, she is, very fond, the doll 等ハ急速ニ續ケテ讀ムコト

（9） am ハ is, are ト同意義ナルモ I ノ後ニノミ之ヲ用フルコト

（10） has ハ have ト同意義ナルモ各其ノ用ヒラルヽ場合ノ異ナルヲ注意記憶スベキコト

讀方ハ

(61)

(1)　Are⌢you a⌢boy'?

(2)　Yes', I *am* a⌢boy`.

(3)　Are⌢*you* also a⌢boy'?

(4)　No', I⌢am *not* a⌢boy`.

(5)　I⌢am a⌢*girl*`.

(6)　The⌢boy has a⌢gun`.

(7)　He⌢is very⌢proud of the⌢gun`.

(8)　The⌢girl has a⌢doll`.

(9)　She⌢is very⌢fond of the⌢doll`.

譯解ハ

(1)　汝ハ(一ノ)男兒デアルカ

(2)　然リ余ハ(一ノ)男兒デアル

(3)　汝モ亦(一ノ)男兒デアルカ

(4)　否余ハ(一ノ)男兒デナイ

(5)　私ハ(一ノ)女兒デアル

(6)　男兒ハ(一ノ)鐵砲ヲ有ツ

(7)　彼ハ鐵砲ヲ甚ダ誇ツテ居ル

(8)　女兒ハ(一ノ)人形ヲ有ツ

(9)　彼女ハ人形ヲ甚ダ好ンデ居ル

　5.　十二新語ノ發音及ビ譯解ノ練習ヲナサシメ次ニ
本課九文章ノ讀方及ビ譯解ヲ練習セシム

(62)

6. 綴方

bake, cake, lake, make, rake, sake, take.

bee, fee, see, deed, heed, keel, meet, need.

先ヅ是等ノ單語ノ發音ヲ聞キテ綴字ヲナサシメ次ニ
綴字ヲ示シテ發音ヲナサシムベシ

7. 書方

The boy has a gun, but the girl has a doll. Please show me the gun and the doll.

是等ノ文章ノ讀方及ビ譯解ヲナサシムベシ

讀方ハ

The⌒boy has a⌒gun′, but the⌒girl has a⌒doll`.
Please show⌒me the⌒gun and the⌒doll`.

譯解ハ

男兒ハ (一ノ) 鐵砲ヲ有ツ併シ女兒ハ (一ノ) 人形ヲ有
ツ、ドーゾ鐵砲ト人形ヲ土見セ下サイ、

(63)

第 十 五 課

I. 復習

A, B, C, D, E, F, H, I, J, M, N, O, P, Q, R, S, T, U, W, Y.

a, b, c, d, e, f, g, h, i, j, k, l, m, n, o, p, q, r, s, t, u, v, w, x, y.

à, go͝od, thē, bŏx, Jŏhn's, ŏf, dǫ, yǫu̇rs, sēę, mȳ, ŏ'pęn, whạt, tākę, gŭn, rēạd'ēr, quītę, hĭṣ, châir, whērę, rĕd, bĕnch, hăṣ, căn, māẏ, proud, thănk, ĭṣn't, sȯmę, ôr, ạlsŏ, to͞o, boy, ärę, rīght, shōw, new, pu̇t, vĕr'ẏ, gīrl, shē, Eng'lĭsh, pĕn'knifę.

Are⌢you a⌢little girl′ ?

Yes′, I *am* a⌢very little girl‵.

You are a⌢big boy‵.

I am *not* a⌢big boy‵.

The⌢boy is proud of⌢his gun‵.

The⌢girl is very⌢fond of that doll‵.

ten, men, hit, pit, bo, no, cat, fat, look, took, but, nut, big, gig, lake, rake, deed, keel.

John's cap is just like Roy's cap. Frank's penknife must be in that box. Have you a pencil? Open the First English Reader. Shut it. Quite right. Very good. Please show me the gun and the doll.

2. 圖畫ニヨリ二人ノ男兒ト二人ノ女兒トヲ全級ノ生徒ニ示シ

Look at the boys and girls.

ト云ヒ其ノ中一人ノ男兒ニ向ヒ

What is your name?

ト問ヒ其ノ男兒ニ代リテ

My name is George.

ト答フ是ニ於テ

George is a good name.

ト云フ。次ニ一人ノ女兒ヲ指サシナガラ

What is her name?

ト問ヒ

(65)

Her name is Kate.

ト答フ。此ノ時

Is Kate a bad name？

ト問ヒ

No, it is not a bad name.

ト答フ。次ニ尚一人ノ男兒ヲ指サシテ

This boy's name is Kinzō.

ト云フ。又尚一人ノ女兒ヲ指サシテ

That girl's name is Ume.

ト云フ。斯ノ如クスルコト數回ニ及ビ生徒ヲシテ其ノ
大意ヲ悟ラシメ更ニ各文章ノ意義ヲ説明シテ此ノ會話
ヲ繰返シ次ノ諸點ヲ敎フ

(1) look ノ ŏŏ ハ book ノ ŏŏ 及ビ pu̯t ノ u̯ ト同音
ナルコト

(2) ăt, băd ノ ă ハ ăn, căn, hăt, hăs ノ ă ト同音ナ
ルコト

(3) boys, girls ノ s ハ z ト發音スルヨリモ s ト發音
スルヲ可トスルコト

(4) nāme̯, Kāte̯ ノ ā ハ tāke̯ ノ ā ト同音ナルコト

(5) George ノ中ニアル母音ハ ôr ノ ô ト同ジキコト

(6) hĕr ノ ĕr ハ fĭrst, gĭrl ノ ĭr ト同ジキコト

(66)

(7)　Kinzō, Ume ハ所謂羅馬字綴ニシテ其ノ母音 I, ō, u, ĕ ハ日本語ノい, をー, う, えナルコト

(8)　look, at, boys, girls, name, George, Kate, bad 等ノ語尾ハ子音ナレバ母音ヲ附加セザルコト

3.　成ルベク多數ノ生徒ヲシテ圖畫ニヨリ本課十文章ノ發音及ビ譯解ヲ試ミシメ若シ誤謬アル時ハ一々丁寧ニ之ヲ訂正ス

4.　次ニ此ノ十文章ヲ順次黑板ニ書キ反復其ノ讀方及ビ譯解ヲ敎ヘ次ノ諸點ヲ說明ス

(1)　look ハ lōok ニアラズシテ lŏok ナルコト

(2)　George ヲげをるじナドト讀マズシテ Jərj トスルコト

(3)　her ヲはー又ハほるトナサザルコト

(4)　bǎd ノ母音 ǎ ヲ明示シばっどト發音セザル樣注意スルコト

(5)　Kinzō, Ume ノ如キ日本ノ人名又ハ物名ガ英文ノ中ニ現ハルル時ハ便宜上已ムヲ得ズ accent ヲ附スルコト又槪シテ penult ニ此ノ accent ヲ置クコト

(6)　疑問ノ種類ニヨリ末尾ノ音調ヲ或ハ高クシ或ハ低クスルコト

(7)　boys, girls ノ s ハ一人ヨリモ多キコトヲ示スコト

(67)

讀方ハ・

(1) Look⌒at the⌒boys and girls`.

(2) What⌒is your⌒name`?

(3) My⌒name is *George*`.

(4) George is a⌒good name`.

(5) What⌒is her⌒name`?

(6) Her⌒name is *Kate*`.

(7) Is Kate a⌒bad name'?

(8) No', it⌒is *not* a⌒bad name`.

(9) This⌒boy's name is Kinzō`.

(10) That⌒girl's name is Ume`.

譯解ハ

(1) 男兒(等)ト女兒(等)トヲ御覽

(2) 汝ノ名ハ何デアルカ

(3) 余ガ名ハじょるじデアル

(4) じょるじハ(一ノ)良イ名デアル

(5) 彼女ノ名ハ何デアルカ

(6) 彼女ノ名ハけーいとデアル

(7) けーいとハ(一ノ)惡イ名デアルカ

(8) 否ソレハ(一ノ)惡イ名デナイ

(9) 此ノ男兒ノ名ハ金藏デアル

(68)

（10）　彼ノ女兒ノ名ハ梅デアル

次ニ五新文字ノ名稱及發音ヲ示シ L, G, K, U ハ l, g, k, u ノ頭文字ナルコトヲ敎フ

五新文字ノ名稱ハ次ノ如シ

L＝ĕl　　　　U＝ゆ～

G＝jee　　　z＝zee 又ハ zĕd

K＝けーい

5.　五新字ノ名稱及ビ發音ト十新語ノ發音及ビ譯解トノ練習ヲナサシメ次ニ本課十文章ノ讀方及譯解ヲ練習セシム

6.　綴 字

dew, few, hew, mew, new, pew, yew, chew.

先ヅ是等ノ單語ノ發音ヲ聞キテ綴字ヲナサシメ次ニ綴字ヲ示シテ發音ヲナサシムベシ

7.　書 方

Boys and girls.　Look at George, Kate, Kinzo, and Ume.　Kate is a very good name.

是等ノ文章ノ讀方及ビ譯解ヲナサシムベシ

(69)

讀方ハ

Boys and girls.` Look⌒at George', Kate',
Kinzō', and Ume.` Kate is a⌒very good name.`

譯解ハ

男兒（等）ト女兒（等）ト、じょるじ、けーいと、金藏
及ビ梅ヲ御覽、けーいとハ（一ノ）甚ダ良イ名デアル、

––––––––––

第 十 六 課

I. 復 習

A, B, C, D, E, F, G, H, I, J, K, L, M, N, O, P,
Q, R, S, T, U, V, W, Y.

a, b, c, d, e, f, g, h, i, j, k, l, m, n, o, p, q, r, s, t,
u, v, w, x, y, z.

a̤, lŏŏk, ē, bŏx, Jŏḥn's, ŏf, do̤, yo̤ṳrs, sēe̤, mȳ,
ō'pe̤n,, wha̤t, nāme̤, gŭn, rēa̤d'ēr, quīte̤, hĭṣ, châir,
whêre̤, rĕd, bĕnch, bă̇d, că̇n, māẏ, proud, thănk,
ĭṣn't, so̤me̤, ôr, a̤l'sō̤, tō̤o, boys, äre̤, rīgḥt, shōẇ, new,
pṳt, vĕr'ẏ, gĭrls, hēr, shē, Georg̣e̤, Eng'lĭsh,
pĕn'ķnīfe̤.

(70)

Look⌒at his gun and her doll .

What⌒is that⌒boy's name˅?

That⌒boy's name is George˅.

She has the⌒First English Reader˅.

His penknife is on the⌒box˅.

Kinzō's cap is *not* like Ume's cap˅.

hen, den, sit, fit, go, so, mat, rat, cook, nook, hut, rut, dig, pig, make, sake, heel, deep, mew, yew.

Frank's penknife must be in that box. Have you a pencil? Open the First English Reader. Shut it. Quite right. Very good. Please show me the gun and the doll. Look at George, Kate, Kinzō, and Ume.

2. あるふぁべっとノ表ヲ全級ノ生徒ニ示シナガラ

Do you know what this is?

ト問ヒ

(71)

This is the English alphabet.

ト答フ。又全表ノ文字ヲ指サシナガラ

Can you read all the letters?

ト問ヒ

Yes, I can.

ト答フ。次ニ小文字ノ部分ヲ示シナガラ

Some of them are small letters.

ト云ヒ又頭文字ノ部分ヲ示シナガラ

Some of them are large letters.

ト云フ。次ニ

What are the large letters called?

ト問ヒ

They are called " Capital Letters."

ト答フ。終リニ

Can you write all these letters?

ト問ヒ

I think I can.

ト答フ。斯ノ如クスルコト數回ニ及ビ生徒ヲシテ其ノ
大意ヲ悟ラシメ更ニ各文章ノ意義ヲ説明シテ此ノ會話
ヲ繰返シ次ノ諸點ヲ教フ

　(1)　know ノ母音ハ show ノ母音ト同ジキコト

(72)

(2) ăl′phȧbĕt ノ ăl ヲ高調ニスルコト

(3) ạll, smạll, cạlled ノ ạ ハ ôr ノ ô 及 ạlso ノ ạ ト 同音ナルコト

(4) lĕt′ters ノ前半 lĕt ヲ高調ニスルコト及ビ後半 tĕrs ノ母音ハ gĭrl, hĕr ノ母音ト同ジキコト

(5) them, they, these ノ th ハ the, this, that ノ th ト同音ナルコト

(6) lärgẹ ノ母音ハ äre ノ母音ト同ジキコト

(7) căp′ĭtȧl ノ căp ヲ高調ニスルコト

(8) they ノ母音ハ tāke, Kāte, nāme 等ノ ā ト同音ナルコト

(9) alphabet ノ pha ト Capital ノ al トニ於ケル母音ハ ȧ ナルコト

(10) wrīte ノ ī ハ Ī, mīne, līke, quīte, rīght 等ノ ī ト同音ナルコト

(11) think ノ th ハ the ノ th ト同種類ノ音ナレドモ 唯前者ハ清音ニシテ後者ハ濁音ナルコト

3. 成ルベク多數ノ生徒ヲシテあるふぁべっとノ表ニ由リ本課十文章ノ發音及ビ譯解ヲ試ミシメ若シ誤謬アル時ハ一々丁寧ニ之ヲ訂正ス

4. 次ニ此ノ十文章ヲ順次黒板ニ書キ反復其ノ讀方及ビ譯解ヲ敎ヘ次ノ諸點ヲ說明ス

(73)

(1) know ノ k 及 w ハ發音セザルコト

(2) alphabet ノ ph ハ f ト同音ナルコト又此ノ如ク長キ語ハ十分時間ヲ取リテ緩々ト發音スルコト

(3) letters ニ二箇ノ t 文字アレドモれったーす ト云ハズ唯れたーす トシテれノ處ヲ高調ニスルコト

(4) small ノ s ト m トノ間ニ母音ヲ挿入セザルコト

(5) large ノ g ハ George ノ g ト同音ナルコト

(6) called ノ l 音ト d 音トノ間ニ母音ヲ挿入セザルコト

(7) they ハ thā ナルコト

(8) write ノ w ハ發音セザルコト

(9) alphabet, all, them, small, large, called, capital, write, these, think ノ末尾ニ母音ヲ加ヘザルコト

(10) letters ノ s ハ一箇ヨリモ多キコトヲ示スコト

(11) them, they ハ it ト同様ノ意義ナレドモ it ハ其ノ代表スルモノ唯一箇ノミノ時ニシテ them, they ハ一箇ヨリモ多キ時用ヒラルヽコト

(12) 第一ノ文章中 what ヲ包含スレドモ Do you know ヲ以テ始マレルガ故ニ矢張末尾ノ音調ヲ高クスルコト

(13) "Capital Letters" ノ " " ハ Inverted Commas 又ハ Quotation Marks ト稱フルモノニテ此ノ處ニテハ

特殊ノ名稱ヲ示スタメノ符號トシテ用ヒラルヽコト

あるふぁべっとノ表ニ由リ頭文字ノ印刷體及ビ草書體ヲ示シ次ニ小文字ノ印刷體及ビ草書體ヲ示シ其ノ名稱及ビ發音ヲ幾回モ練習スベシ。本課ニ於テ新シキ文字ハ印刷體ノ X, Z ト草書體ノ *X, Z* トニシテ x, z ノ頭文字ナリ

二新字ノ名稱ハ

X＝ĕx　　　　　　Z＝zee 又ハ zĕd

5. あるふぁべっと 二十六字ノ名稱及ビ發音ト十三新語ノ發音及び譯解トノ練習ヲナサシメ次ニ本課十文章ノ讀方及ビ譯解ヲ練習セシム

6. 綴 字

ink, bink, link, pink, sink, chink, think.

先ヅ是等ノ單語ノ發音ヲ聞キテ 綴字ヲナサシメ次ニ綴字ヲ示シテ發音ヲナサシムベシ

7. 書 方

X and Z are new letters. Can you write all the English letters? I think I can. Write them now.

是等ノ文章ノ讀方及ビ譯解ヲナサシムベシ

(75)

讀方ハ

X and Z are new letters`.   Can⌢you write all
⌢the⌢English letters`?   I think I *can*`. · Write them
now`.

譯解ハ

X ト Z トハ新シキ文字デアル、汝ハ總ベテノ英字ヲ
書クコトガ出來ルカ、余ハ出來ルト思フ、サアソレヲ
書ケ、

第　十　七　課

Ⅰ 復 習

à, lŏŏk, thĕm, bŏx, Jŏhn's, ŏf, do, yoụrs, sēẹ, mȳ,
ō'pẹn, whạt, nāmẹ, gŭn, rēạd'ēr, quītẹ, hĭş, châir,
whêrẹ, bĕnch, căn, māẙ, proud, thĭnk, ĭşn't, sómẹ,
ôr, ạl'sō, tōō, boys, lärġẹ, rīghֵt, ƙnōẘ, new, pụt,
vĕr'ẙ, gĭrls, hĕr, shē, Georġẹ, smạll, theẙ, ẘrītẹ,
Eng'lĭsh, lĕt'tērs, ăl'phàbĕt, căp'ĭtàl.

Can⌢you write the⌢English alphabet`?

Yes,′ I can write all these letters`.

(76)

The⌒large letters are⌒called " Capital Letters`."

Can⌒you read the⌒First English Reader'?

I think I *can*`.

Some of⌒these boys are bad boys`.

Some of⌒them are good girls`.

ken, ten, hit pit, bo, no, cat, fat, good, look, but, gut, big, rig, cake, snake, feel, deed, new, chew, link, sink.

Have you a pencil? Open the First English Reader. Shut it. Quite right. Very good. Please show me the gun and the doll. Look at George, Kate, Kinzō, and Ume. I think I can write all the English letters.

2. 全級ノ生徒ニ向ヒ手眞似及ビ身振ヲ用ヒ又ハ圖畫ニヨリテ

Stand up.

(77)

Stand up and come here.

ト云ヒ立チ上ガラザル生徒ニ向ヒ

Why do you not stand up?

ト問ヒ其ノ生徒ニ代リテ身振ヲ用ヒテ

I stand up and go there.

ト答フ。其ノ生徒來リタル時彼ニ向ヒ手眞似ヲ以テ

Now, you are here.

ト云フ。次ニ手眞似ヲ用ヒテ

Go to the door.

ト云ヒ戸ニ達セシ時手眞似ヲ用ヒテ

Please open the door.

ト云フ。生徒之ヲ聞キタル後又手眞似ヲ用ヒテ

Shut it, please.

ト云フ。畢テ手眞似ヲ用ヒナガラ

Go back to your seat.

ト云ヒ生徒其ノ席ニ達シタル時手眞似及ビ身振ヲ添ヘ
テ

Sit down.

ト云フ。又更ニ

Did you sit down?

ト問ヒ生徒ニ代リテ

(78)

Yes, I did.

ト答フ。斯ノ如クスルコト數回ニ及ビ生徒ヲシテ其ノ大意ヲ悟ラシメ更ニ各文章ノ意義ヲ説明シテ 此ノ會話ヲ繰返シ次ノ諸點ヲ教フ

(1) stand, back ノ母音ハ căn, băg, blăck ノ母音ト同音ナルコト

(2) cȯme ノ ȯ ハ sȯme ノ ȯ 又ハ bŭt, ŭp ノ ŭ ト同音ナルコト

(3) whȳ ノ ȳ ハ mȳ ノ ȳ 又ハ mīne, quīte ノ ī ト同音ナルコト

(4) gō, dōọr ノ母音ハ nō, ōld ノ ō ト同音ナルコト

(5) tọ ハ tōō ト同音ナルコト

(6) now ノ ow ハ down ノ ow 又ハ proud ノ ou ト同音ナルコト

(7) seat ノ母音ハ read ノ母音ト同ジキコト

(8) did ノ母音ハ it, is, big ノ母音ト同ジキコト

3. 成ルベク多數ノ生徒ヲシテ手眞似及ビ身振ニ由リ又ハ圖畫ニヨリ本課十二文章ノ發音及ビ譯解ヲ試ミシメ若シ誤謬アル時ハ一々丁寧ニ之ヲ訂正ス

4. 次ニ此ノ十二文章ヲ順次黑板ニ書キ 反復其ノ讀方及ビ譯解ヲ教ヘ次ノ諸點ヲ説明ス

(1) cȯme ノ e ハ發音セザルコト又 ȯ ハ ŭ ノ音ナル

（ 79 ）

コト

（2） to ノ o ハ do ノ o ト同ジクオーラ ニアラズ
シテラーナルコト

（3） door ノ oo ハ ラーニアラズシテオーラナルコト

（4） stand, come, back, seat, did ノ末尾ニ母音ヲ加
ヘザルコト

（5） do ハ現在ヲ示シ did ハ過去ヲ示スコト

讀方ハ

　(1)　Stand⌢up`.

　(2)　Stand⌢up and come⌢here`.

　(3)　Why do⌢you not stand⌢up`?

　(4)　I stand⌢up and go⌢there`.

　(5)　Now′, you⌢are here`.

　(6)　Go to the⌢door`.

　(7)　Please open the⌢door`.

　(8)　Shut⌢it, please`.

　(9)　Go⌢back to your⌢seat`.

　(10)　Sit⌢down`.

　(11)　Did⌢you sit⌢down′?

　(12)　Yes′, I did`.

(80)

譯解ハ

(1)　立チ上レ

(2)　立チ上リテ茲ニ來レ

(3)　ナゼ汝ハ立チ上ラヌカ

(4)　余ハ立チ上リテ其所ニ行ク

(5)　ソレ汝ハ茲ニ居ル

(6)　戸ノ所ニ行ケ

(7)　ドーゾ戸ヲ今開キナサイ

(8)　ソレヲ今閉ヂナサイ、ドーゾ、

(9)　汝ノ席ニ歸レ

(10)　坐レ

(11)　汝ハ坐ッタカ

(12)　然リ余ハ坐ッタ

5.　十新語ノ發音及ビ譯解ノ練習ヲナサシメ次ニ本課十二文章ノ讀方及ビ譯解ヲ練習セシム

6.　綴字

ate, date, fate, gate, hate, late, mate, pate, rate, sate, slate, grate, state.

先ヅ是等ノ單語ノ發音ヲ聞キテ綴字ヲナサシメ次ニ綴字ヲ示シテ發音ヲナサシムベシ

7.　書方

(81)

Why do you not stand up and open the door? Go back to your seat, and sit down.

是等ノ文章ノ讀方及ビ譯解ヲナサシムベシ

讀方ハ

Why do⌒you not stand⌒*up* and open the⌒door`?
Go⌒*back* to your⌒seat', and sit⌒*down*.`

譯解ハ

ナゼ汝ハ立チ上リテ戸ヲ開カヌカ、汝ノ席ニ歸リテ
坐レ

第　十　八　課

本課ハ第一課ヨリ第十七課マデニ敎ヘタル所ヲ復習
セシムルモノナレバ一字一語又一音タリトモ未ダ記憶
セザルモノアラバ決シテ次課ニ進ムベカラズ

1. 頭文字　二十六箇　印刷體及草書體

各字ノ名稱及ビ發音ヲ練習セシメ又種々ノ　小文字ヲ
示シテ之ニ對スル頭文字ヲ答ヘシメ次ニ此ノ二十六箇
頭文字ノ書方ヲ練習セシム

2. 小文字　二十六箇　印刷體及ビ草書體

（ 82 ）

　各字ノ名稱及ビ發音ヲ練習セシメ又種々ノ頭文字ヲ
示シテ之ニ對スル小文字ヲ答ヘシメ次ニ 此二十六箇小
文字ノ書方ヲ練習セシム

　3. 母音　十九個

　是ハ文字ニヨラズシテ唯聲音ノミヲ敎フルノ 目的ナ
レバ ôr ノ ô ハ ạ ノ中ニ入リ fĭrst, gĭrl ノ ĭ ハ ẽ ノ中
ニ入リ everў ノ ў ハ ĭ ノ中ニ入リ whạt ノ ạ ハ ŏ ノ中
ニ入リ sòme, còme ノ ò ハ ŭ ノ中ニ入リ dọ, tọ ノ ọ ハ
ōō ノ中ニ入リ pụt ノ ụ ハ ŏŏ ノ中ニ入リ thêre, whêre
ノ ê ハ â ノ中ニ入リ theỵ ノ ẹ 又 may ノ ay ハ ā ノ中
ニ入リ see ノ ee 又 read, seat ノ ea ハ ē ノ中ニ入リ
show, know ノ ow 又 door ノ oo ハ ō ノ中ニ入リ new
ノ ew ハ ū ノ中ニ入リ Roy, boy ノ oy ハ oi ノ中ニ入
リ down, now ノ ow ハ ou ノ中ニ入ルナリ。先ヅ此ノ
十九箇母音ノ練習ヲナシ各母音ヲ含メル 單語ヲ擧ゲシ
ム

　4. 子音　二十六箇

　是モ文字ニヨラズシテ唯聲音ノミヲ敎フルノ 目的ナ
レバ ph ハ f ノ中ニ入リ George, large ノ g ハ j ノ中
ニ入リ of ノ f ハ v ノ中ニ入リ is, has, his 等ノ s ハ z
ノ中ニ入リ r (initial) ト r (final) ト ヲ區別シ wh, th, ch,
ng, sh, qu 等ヲモ含ミ th ト th ト ヲ區別ス。先ヅ此ノ二

(83)

十六箇子音ノ練習ヲナシ各子音ヲ含メル單語ヲ擧ゲシ
ム

6. 單語　百二十八個

各單語ノ發音及ビ譯解ヲ練習シ次ニ各單語ヲ含メル
句又ハ文章ヲ擧ゲシム

5. 本課十二文章ノ讀方又譯解ヲ練習シ殊ニ音調ノ
接續及ビ抑揚ニ注意スベシ又成ルベク直譯ノ弊ヲ避ケ
テ純良ナル日本文ニ譯スベシ

讀方ハ

   (1)　Did⌢you open the⌢door'?

   (2)　Yes', I⌢*did*`.

   (3)　Who *are*⌢you`?

   (4)　I⌢am *Frank*`.

   (5)　John is a⌢bad boy', but Kate is a⌢good
       girl`.

   (6)　Have⌢you red ink'?

   (7)　No', I⌢have *black* ink`.

   (8)　Stand⌢*up* and read the⌢book`.

   (9)　Can⌢you write the⌢alphabet'?

  (10)　Yes', I⌢*can*`.

  (11)　What⌢are the⌢Capital Letters`?

(84)

(12) They‿are the‿large letters`.

譯解ハ

(1) 汝ハ戸ヲ開イタカ

(2) 然リ余ハ開イタ

(3) 汝ハ誰カ

(4) 余ハふらんくデアル

(5) じょんハ(一ノ)惡シキ男兒デアルガけいとハ(一ノ)善キ女兒デアル

(6) 汝ハ赤いんきヲ有ツカ

(7) 否余ハ黒いんきヲ有ツ

(8) 立チ上リテ書物ヲ讀〆

(9) 汝ハあるふぁべっとヲ書クコトガ出來ルカ

(10) 然リ余ハ出來ル

(11) 頭文字トハ何デアルカ

(12) ソレハ大文字デアル

7. 綴字

fight, light, might, night, right, sight, tight, slight.

先ヅ是等ノ單語ノ發音ヲ聞キテ綴字ヲナサシメ次ニ綴字ヲ示シテ發音ヲナサムベシ

8. 書方

(85)

Can you write the alphabet?
Yes, I can. What are the Capital
Letters? They are large letters.
Stand up and read the book.

是等ノ文章ノ讀方及ビ譯解ヲナサシムベシ

讀方ハ

Can⌒you write the⌒alphabet′?　Yes′, I *can*`.
What⌒are the⌒Capital Letter`?　They⌒are the⌒
large letters`.　Stand⌒*up* and read the⌒book`.

譯解ハ

汝ハ あるふぁべっと ヲ書クコトガ出來ルカ.　然リ余
ハ出來ル.　頭文字トハ何デアルカ.　ソレハ大文字デア
ル.　立チ上リテ書物ヲ讀メ.

第　十　九　課

1. 復習

(1)　Frank's⌒chair is a⌒very good chair`.

(2)　Please show⌒me your pencil and penknife`.

(3)　I⌒think you⌒know all these letters`.

(86)

(4)   Is⌢it also *black* ink'?

(5)   No', *red*⌢ink is in this⌢inkstand'.

(6)   What have⌢you in the⌢bag'?

(7)   I⌢have the⌢First English Reader *in*⌢it'.

(8)   Where⌢is your⌢cap'?

(9)   My⌢cap is on the⌢*table* there'.

(10)   Whose⌢doll *is*⌢this'?

(11)   I⌢think it⌢is *Ume's* doll'.

(12)   Why do⌢you not stand⌢*up* and come here'?

pen, den, lit, sit, ho, lo, pat, sat, foot, took, hut, rut, dig, fig, bake, lake, keel, meet, dew, few, chink, pink, slate, grate, right, tight.

Please show me the gun and the doll. Look at George, Kate, Kinzō, and Ume. I think I can write all the English letters. Why do you not go back to your seat and

(87)

sit down? The large letters are called "Capital Letters."

2. 實物又ハ圖畫ニ由リ先ヅ紙ヲ全級ノ生徒ニ示シテ

Who wants this paper?

ト問ヒ生徒ニ代リテ

I want it.

ト答ヘ又いんきヲ指シテ

Whose ink is this?

ト問ヒ生徒ニ代リテ

It is our teacher's.

ト答フ。次ニぺんヲ示シナガラ

Is this your pen, John?

ト問ヒじょんニ代リテ

No, it is Frank's.

ト答フ。扨二種ノ紙ヲ比較シナガラ

This paper is thick, but that paper is thin.

ト云ヒ次ニ自分ノ赤いんきト生徒ノ黒いんきトヲ比較シテ

Your ink is black, but my ink isrd.

(88)

ト云フ。後生徒ニ代リテ

We have some thick paper and black ink.

ト云ヒ又

Our teacher has some thin paper and red ink.

ト云ヒ生徒ニ代リテ

May I write on this paper?

ト問ヒ

Yes, you may.

ト答フ

斯ノ如クスルコト数回ニ及ビ生徒ヲシテ 其ノ大意ヲ悟ラシメ更ニ文章ノ意義ヲ說明シテ此ノ會話ヲ繰返シ次ノ諸點ヲ敎フ

(1) who ノ o ハ do, to ノ o ト同音ナルコト及ビ fōō ニアラズシテ hōō ナルコト

(2) want ノ a ハ all ノ a ト同音ナレバ wănt, wànt, wŏnt, wônt 等ト混ズベカラザルコト

(3) pā'pĕr, tēăch'ĕr ノ後半ニ於ケル母音ハ gĭrl, hĕr 等ニ於ケル母音ト同ジキコト

(4) our ノ母音ハ proud, down ノ母音ト同ジキコト

(5) thĭck, thĭn ノ th ハ清音ナルコト

(6) want, we ノ w ハ日本語ノわノ字ヲ發音スル時ニ於ケル脣ノ形ヲナシテ發音スルコト

(89)

3. 成ルベク多數ノ生徒ヲシテ 實物又ハ圖畵ヲ用ヒ
テ本課十二文章ノ發音及ビ譯解ヲ 試ミシメ若シ誤謬ア
ル時ハ一々丁寧ニ之ヲ訂正ス

4. 次ニ此ノ十二文章ヲ 順次黑板ニ書キ反復其ノ讀
方及ビ譯解ヲ敎ヘ次ノ諸點ヲ說明ス

(1) who ノ wh ハ what, where, which ノ wh ト異ナ
リ單ニ h ト同音ナルコト

(2) pā′pĕr, tēₐch′ĕr ノ前半ヲ高調ニスルコト

(3) want, thick ノ末尾ニ母音ヲ加ヘザルコト

讀方ハ

(1) Who wants this paper`?

(2) *I* want⌢it`.

(3) Whose⌢ink *is*⌢this`?

(4) It⌢is our *teacher's*`.

(5) Is⌢this your *pen*, John′?

(6) No′, it⌢is *Frank's*`.

(7) *This*⌢paper is *thick*′, but *that*⌢paper is *thin*`.

(8) *Your*⌢ink is *black*′, but *my*⌢ink is *red*`.

(9) We have some thick⌢paper and black⌢ink`.

(10) Our teacher has some thin⌢paper and red⌢
ink`.

(90)

(11)　May⌢I write on this paper′?

(12)　Yes′, you⌢*may*`.

譯解ハ

(1)　誰ガ此ノ紙ヲ欲シイカ

(2)　余ハソレヲ欲シイ

(3)　是ハ誰レノいんきデアルカ

(4)　ソレハ我等ノ先生ノデアル

(5)　じょんヨ是ハ汝ノぺんデアルカ

(6)　否ソレハふらんくノデアル

(7)　此ノ紙ハ厚イガ其ノ紙ハ薄イ

(8)　汝ノいんきハ黒イガ余ノいんきハ赤イ

(9)　我等ハ多少ノ厚紙ト黒いんきトヲ有ツ

(10)　我等ノ先生ハ多少ノ薄紙ト赤いんきトヲ有ツ

(11)　余ハ此ノ紙ニ書イテ可イカ

(12)　然リ、可シ

　5.　ハ新語ノ發音及ビ譯解ノ練習ヲナサシメ 次ニ本
課十二文章ノ讀方及ビ譯解ヲ練習セシム

　6.　綴字

　bow, cow, how, now, down, gown, town, fair,
hair, lair, pair, chair.

　先ヅ是等ノ單語ノ發音ヲ聞キテ綴字ヲナサシメ 次ニ
綴字ヲ示シテ發音ヲナサシムベシ

(91)

7. 書方

*John's paper and Frank's ink.
The teacher has a pen, but we have
pencils. Who wants this paper?*

是等ノ文章ノ讀方及ビ譯解ヲナサシムベシ

讀方ハ

John's paper and Frank's ink`. The⌒teacher
has a⌒*pen'*, but *we* have *pencils*`. Who wants this
paper`?

譯解ハ

じょんノ紙トふらんくノいんきト。 先生ハ一本ノペ
んヲ有ツガ我等ハ鉛筆ヲ有ツ。 誰ガ此ノ紙ヲ欲シイ
カ。

_____

第 二 十 課

1. 復習

a̍, loŏk, thĕm, bŏx, Jŏhn's, ŏf, who̧, yo̧u̧rs, sēȩ,
whȳ, ō'pȩn, wha̧t, nāmȩ, gŭn, tēa̧ch'ēr, quitȩ, hĭs̱,
châir, whêrȩ, bĕnch, co̧mȩ, māy̱, our, thĭnk, ĭs̱n't,

(92)

ôr, ạl'sŏ, tōō, boys, lärg̣ẹ, rīg̣ht, ḳnōẉ, new, pụt,
vĕr'ÿ, gīrls, hēr, shē, George, thẹẙ, ẉrītẹ, dōọr,
wạnt, Eng'lĭsh, lĕt'tērs, ăl'phȧbĕt, căp'ĭtȧl.

Who wants this penknife˅?

We do not *want*⌒it˅.

Whose paper is⌒that˅?

That⌒is our *teacher's* paper˅.

George is quite proud of⌒his gun˅.

Kate is very⌒fond of⌒her doll˅.

men, wren, wit, flit, go, old, bat, flat, nook,
stood, nut, glut, pig, twig, wake, shake, heel, sweet,
pew, stew, wink, brink, mate, state, sight, bright,
how, gown, hair, pair.

*Look at George, Kate, Kinzō,
and Ume. I think I can write
all the English letters. Why do you
not go back to your seat and sit
down? The large letters are called*

(93)

*"Capital Letters."   Our teacher has
pen, but we have pencils.*

2. 全級ノ生徒ニ自分ノ顔ヲ示シナガラ 手眞似ヲ用
ヒテ

Look at my face.

ト云ヒ口鼻目耳ヲ指シナガラ其ノ數ヲモ示シテ

I have one mouth and one nose.

There are two eyes and two ears.

ト云ヒ次ニ生徒ニ向ヒテ

How many mouths have you?

ト問ヒ生徒ニ代リテ手眞似ヲ用ヒナガラ

I have one mouth.

ト答ヘ又

How many eyes have I?

ト問ヒ生徒ニ代リテ手眞似ヲ用ヒナガラ

You have two eyes.

ト答フ。次ニ

What are the eyes for?

ト問ヒ

We see with the eyes.

（ 94 ）

ト答ヘ之ト同樣ニ

What are the ears for?

We hear with the ears.

ノ問答ヲナス。斯ノ如クスルコト數回ニ及ビ生徒ヲシテ其ノ大意ヲ悟ラシメ更ニ各文章ノ意義ヲ說明シテ此ノ會話ヲ繰返シ次ノ諸點ヲ敎フ

(1)　one ノ發音ハ wŭn ナルコト

(2)　mouth, how ノ母音ハ now, proud ノ母音ト同ジキコト

(3)　mouth ノ th ハ thin, thick ノ th ノ如ク清音ニシテ明瞭ニ發音スベキコト

(4)　mouths ハ mouthz ナルコト

(5)　noṣe ノ ṣ ハ z ノ音ナルコト

(6)　two ハ tōō ト同音ナルコト

(7)　fôr ノ ô ハ ôr ノ ô 又 all ノ ạ ト同音ナルコト

(8)　with ノ th ハ濁音ニシテ the, this, that ノ th ト同ジキコト

3. 成ルベク多數ノ生徒ヲシテ本課十一文章ノ發音及ビ譯解ヲ試ミシメ若シ誤謬アル時ハ一々丁寧ニ之ヲ訂正ス

4. 次ニ此ノ十一文章ヲ順次黑板ニ書キ反復其ノ讀方及ビ譯解ヲ敎ヘ次ノ諸點ヲ說明ス

(95)

(1) façe ノ ç ハ pençil ノ ç ト同ジク s ノ音ナルコト

(2) one ノ發音ハ異例ニシテ最初ニ w ヲ附シ wǔn トナルコト

(3) two ノ發音モ異例ニシテ too ト同ジキコト

(4) eyes ノ發音モ異例ニシテ īs ナルコト

(5) eārs, hēar ノ母音ハ hē, shē ノ ē ニシテ其ノ次ニ r (final) ノ音ヲ附加スルコト

(6) many ノ發音モ頗ル異例ニシテ mě'nǐ ナレバめ ーにートナサザル様注意スベキコト又前半 mě ヲ高調 ニスルコト

(7) face, nose ノ e ハ發音セザルコト

(8) eyes, ears ノ s ハ z トナスヨリモ寧ロ s ノ清音 トナスヲ實際優レリトスルコト

(9) face, mouth, eyes, ears, with ノ末尾ニ母音ヲ附 セザルコト

(10) eyes, ears, mouths ノ s ハ一箇ヨリ多キコトヲ示 スコト

讀方ハ

(1) *Look⌢at my⌢face*`.

(2) I have one *mouth*' and one *nose*`.

(3) There⌢are two *eyes*' and two *ears*`.

(96)

(4) How many *mouths have⌒you*`?

(5) I have *one mouth*`.

(6) How many *eyes have⌒I*`?

(7) You have *two eyes*`.

(8) What are the⌒*eyes* for`?

(9) We *see* with the⌒eyes`.

(10) What are the⌒*ears* for`?

(11) We *hear* with the⌒ears`.

譯解ハ

（1）余ノ顔ヲ御覧

（2）余ハ一箇ノ口ト一箇ノ鼻トヲ有ツ

（3）二箇ノ目ト二箇ノ耳トガアル

（4）汝ハ幾箇ノ口ヲ有ツカ

（5）余ハ一箇ノ口ヲ有ツ

（6）余ハ幾箇ノ目ヲ有ツカ

（7）汝ハ二箇ノ目ヲ有ツ

（8）目ハ何ノ爲デアルカ

（9）我等ハ目ニテ見ル

（10）耳ハ何ノ爲デアルカ

（11）我等ハ耳ニテ聞ク

　5. 十二新語ノ發音及ビ譯解ノ練習ヲナサシメ次ニ本課十一文章ノ讀方及ビ譯解ヲ練習セシム

6. 綴字

boot, cool, doom, fool, loom, moon, noon, pool, root, soot, tool.

先ヅ是等ノ單語ノ發音ヲ聞キテ 綴字ヲナサシメ次ニ 綴字ヲ示シテ發音ヲナサシムベシ

7. 書方

How many eyes have you? I have two eyes. Is my face just like your face? Yes, it is; you are quite right.

是等ノ文章ノ讀方及ビ譯解ヲナサシムベシ

讀方ハ

How many *eyes have* you`?　I have *two eyes*`. Is my`face just like your`face'?　Yes', it is; you` are quite *right*`.

譯解ハ

汝ハ幾箇ノ目ヲ有ツカ、余ハ二個ノ目ヲ有ツ、余ノ 顏ハ丁度汝ノ顏ノ如クアルカ、然リサウデアル、汝ノ 言フ通リ

(98)

第 二 十 一 課

I. 復習

á, loŏk, thĕm, bŏx, Jŏhn's, ŏf, who, yoùrs, sēe̜,
whȳ, ō'pe̜n, whạt, fāçe̜, gŭn, hēạr, quīte̜, nōṣe̜,
châir, whêre̜, bĕnch, cóme̜, māy̆, our, thĭnk, ĭṣn't,
fôr, ạl'sō, tōō, boys, lärge̜, rīght, know̆, new, pụt,
vĕr'y̆, gīrls, hēr, shē, George, they̆, write̜, dōọr,
wạnt, one, two̜, eyes, many, mouthṣ, Eng'lĭsh,
lĕt'tērs, ăl'phạbĕt, căp'ĭtạl.

Please *look*⌢at my face`.

Do⌢you see my two⌢eyes and one⌢nose'?

Yes', I see your two⌢ears and one⌢mouth *too*`.

What⌢is *ink* for`?

We *write* with ink`.

How many books *have*⌢you`?

Not very many`.

glen, spit, hold, spat, crook, shut, wig, prig,
make, quake, keel, fleet, few, knew, bink, stink,

(99)

hate, skate, might, plight, cow, brow, lair, stair, cool, moon.

I think I can write all the English letters. Why do you not go back to your seat and sit down? The large letters are called "Capital Letters." Our teacher has a pen, but we have pencils. How many eyes have you? I have two eyes.

2. 實物又ハ圖畫ニヨリ先ヅ机ヲ全級ノ生徒ニ示シ

What is a desk made of?

ト問ヒ

It is made of wood.

ト答ヘ又書物ヲ示シナガラ

What is a book made of?

ト問ヒ

It is made of paper.

ト答フ次ニ椅子ヲ指シテ

(100)

Is a chair made of wood?

ト問ヒ

Yes, it is.

ト答フ又半靴ヲ示シナガラ

Are shoes made of paper?

ト問ヒ首ヲ振リテ

No, they are not made of paper.

ト答ヘ直ニ

What are they made of?

ト問ヒ

They are made of leather.

ト答ヘ又長靴ヲ指シテ

So are boots.

ト云フ。次ニ長靴ト半靴トヲ指サシナガラ

Both boots and shoes are made of leather.

ト云ヒ最後ニ

Who gave you all these things?

ト問ヒ生徒ニ代リテ

Papa gave them to me.

ト答フ。斯ノ如クスルコト數回ニ及ビ生徒ヲシテ其大
意ヲ悟ラシメ更ニ各文章ノ意義ヲ説明シテ此ノ會話ヲ

（ 101 ）

繰リ返シ次ノ諸點ヲ教フ

(1) mādę, gāvę ノ ā ハ tākę, nāmę, pā'pẽr ノ ā ト
同音ナルコト

(2) wŏŏd ノ母音ハ bŏŏk, gŏŏd ノ ŏŏ ト同音ナルコ
ト又 wŏŏ ハ日本語ニ現存セザルノ音ニシテわゐうゑを
ノう二十分 w 音ヲ冠ラセタルモノナレバうっd ニア
ラズシテ w うっd ナルコト

(3) shoes, boots ノ母音ハ tōō ノ ōō 又 dǫ ノ ǫ ト同
音ナルコト

(4) lĕạth'ẽr ニハ l, th, ẽr ノ如キ日本人ニ困難ナル
音多キガ故ニ特別ニ練習スルコト

(5) sō, bōth ノ母音ハ gō, nō ノ ō ト同ジキコト

(6) things ノ ng ハ鼻音ナルコト

(7) leather ノ th ハ濁音ナレド both, things ノ th ハ
清音ナルコト

(8) pà̀pä' ノ前半ハぱニシテ後半ハぱーナルコト

3. 成ルベク多數ノ生徒ヲシテ實物又ハ圖畫ニヨリ
本課十四文章ノ發音又ハ譯解ヲ試ミシメ若シ誤謬アル
時ハ一々丁寧ニ之ヲ訂正ス

4. 次ニ此ノ十四文章ヲ順次黑板ニ書キ反復其ノ讀
方及ビ譯解ヲ教ヘ次ノ諸點ヲ說明ス

(1) made, shoes, gave ノ e ハ發音セザルコト

(102)

(2) wood ハ wōŏd ニアラズシテ wŏŏd ナルコト

(3) shoes ノ o ヲ ō ト讀マズ又 s ヲ z トナサザルコト

(4) leather ヲ lēther ト讀マザルコト又 lĕặth ヲ高調ニスルコト

(5) bōŏts ノ t ト s トノ間ニ母音ヲ插サマズシテ讀ミ殆ドツニ近キ音ヲ出スコト

(6) things ノ s モ z トナスニ及バザルコト

(7) papa′ ノ後半ヲ高調ニスルコト

(8) shoes, boots ノ s ハ一箇ヨリ多キコトヲ示スコト

(9) 「それは」ト云フ語ハ一箇ナラバ it ニシテ一箇ヨリ多キ時ハ they 又ハ them トナルコト

(10) give ハ現在ヲ示シ gave ハ過去ヲ示スコト

讀方ハ

(1) What⌒is a⌒*desk made*⌒of‵?

(2) It⌒is made of⌒*wood*‵.

(3) What⌒is a⌒*book made*⌒of‵?

(4) It⌒is made of⌒*paper*‵.

(5) Is a⌒*bench* made of⌒*wood*′?

(6) Yes′, it⌒*is*‵.

(103)

(7) Are *shoes* made of ⌢*paper'* ?

(8) No', they⌢are *not* made of⌢paper‵.

(9) What *are*⌢they made⌢of‵ ?

(10) They⌢are made of⌢*leather*‵.

(11) So are *boots*‵.

(12) Both boots and shoes are made of⌢leather‵.

(13) Who *gave* you all these things‵ ?

(14) *Papa gave*⌢them to⌢me‵.

譯解ハ

(1) 机ハ何デ出來テ居ルカ

(2) ソレハ木デ出來テ居ル

(3) 書物ハ何デ出來テ居ルカ

(4) ソレハ紙デ出來テ居ル

(5) 腰掛ハ木デ出來テ居ルカ

(6) 然リサウデアル

(7) 半靴ハ紙デ出來テ居ルカ

(8) 否ソレハ紙デ出來テ居ラヌ

(9) ソレハ何デ出來テ居ルカ

(10) ソレハ革デ出來テ居ル

(11) 長靴モサウデアル

(12) 長靴ト半靴ト兩方ガ革デ出來テ居ル

(104)

（13）　誰ガ惣テ是等ノ物ヲ汝ニ與ヘタカ

（14）　父上ガソレヲ余ニ與ヘタ

5.　十一新語ノ發音及ビ譯解ノ練習ヲナサシメ次ニ本課十四文章ノ讀方及ビ譯解ヲ練習セシム

6.　綴字

thy, they, that, this, **these,** those, **there,** them, then, than.

先ヅ是等ノ單語ノ發音ヲ聞キテ綴字ヲナサシメ次ニ綴字ヲ示シテ發音ヲナサシムベシ

7.　書方

Both the boots and the shoes are made of leather. Who gave you all these things? Papa gave them to me.

是等ノ文章ノ讀方及ビ譯解ヲナサシムベシ

讀方ハ

Both the⌒boots and the⌒shoes are made of⌒leather`. Who *gave*⌒you all these things`? *Papa gave*⌒them to⌒me`.

(105)

譯解ハ

長靴ト半靴ト兩方ガ革デ出來テ居ル、誰ガ總ベテ是
等ノ物ヲ汝ニ與ヘタカ、父上ガソレヲ余ニ與ヘタ。

第 二 十 二 課

I. 復習

pȧpä', woŏd, ŧhĕm, bŏx, Jŏḥn's, ŏf, ẉhọ, yọụrs,
sēȼ, whȳ, ō'pȼn, whȧt, fāçȼ, gŭn, hēȧr, quītȼ,
nōṣȼ, châir, whêrȼ, bĕnch, cómȼ, māy, our, thĭngs,
ĭṣn't, fȯr, ạl'sō, bo͞ots, boys, rĭgḥt, ḳnōẉ, new,
pụt, vĕr'ȳ, gīrls, hēr, mē, George, ŧheẙ, wrītȼ,
dōȯr, wạnt, one, tẉọ, eyes, many, mouŧḥṣ,
Eng'lĭsh, lĕt'tērs, ăl'phȧbĕt, căp'ĭtȧl, lĕȧŧh'ēr.

What⌢is a⌢*chair made*⌢of`?

Do⌢you find boots and shoes'?

This is my new book`.

Papa *gave*⌢me all these things`.

You may take this paper and that pen`.

Thank⌢you`.

(106)

Send, quit, gold, plat, brook, strut, brig, snake,
feed, greed, chew, slew, chink, brink, date, plate,
night, flight, bow, prow, fair, chair, pool, stool,
there, than.

Why do you not go back to your seat and sit down? The large letters are called "Capital Letters." Our teacher has a pen, but we have pencils. How many eyes have you? I have two eyes. Who gave you all these things? Papa gave them to me.

2. 手眞似ヲ用ヒテ生徒ニ向ヒ

Show me your hands.

ト云ヒ手ヲ示シタル時矢張手眞似ヲ用ヒテ

How many fingers have you?

ト問ヒ生徒ニ代リテ手ノ指ヲ数ヘナガラ

I have ten fingers.

ト答ヘ更ニ右ノ手及ビ左ノ手ノ指ヲ順次數ヘナガラ

Five fingers on the right hand, and five ınore on the left.

ト云フ。次ニ圖畫ニヨリ右ノ足ヲ示シテ

This is my right foot.

ト云ヒ又左ノ足ヲ示シテ

This is my left foot.

ト云ヒ更ニ圖畫ニヨリ左右ノ足ノ指ヲ數ヘナガラ

My feet have five toes each.

ト云ヒ次ニ手ノ指ノ爪ヲ示シテ

Each finger has a nail.

ト云ヒ又圖畫ニヨリ足ノ指ノ爪ヲ示シテ

Each toe has a nail.

ト云フ最後ニ兩手ノ指ノ爪ヲ數ヘナガラ

Two hands have ten nails.

ト云ヒ又圖畫ニヨリ兩足ノ指ノ爪ヲ數ヘナガラ

Each foot has five nails.

ト云フ。斯ノ如クスルコト數回ニ及ビ生徒ヲシテ其大意ヲ悟ラシメ更ニ各文章ノ意義ヲ說明シテ此會話ヲ繰返シ次ノ諸點ヲ敎フ

(I) finger ノ ng ハ鼻音ナルコト

（108）

（2） five ノ f ト v トハ類似セル音ニテ殊ニ日本人ニ
容易ナラサル音ナレバ混同セザル樣注意スルコト

（3） mōrẹ ハ maṛ ニアラズシテ mōr ナルコト

（4） fŏŏt ノ母音ハ bŏŏk, lŏŏk ノ母音ト同ジキコト

3. 成ルベク多數ノ生徒ヲシテ實物又ハ圖畫ニヨリ
本課十一文章ノ發音及ビ譯解ヲ試ミシメ若シ誤謬アル
時ハ一々丁寧ニ之ヲ訂正ス

4. 次ニ此ノ十一文章ヲ順次黑板ニ書キ反復其ノ讀
方及ビ譯解ヲ敎ヘ次ノ諸點ヲ說明ス

（1） fĭn'gĕr ノ前半 fĭn ヲ高調ニスルコト

（2） fivẹ ヲ hīv 又ハ fif ト云ハザル樣注意スルコト

（3） fŏŏt ヲ fōōt ト云ハザルコト

（4） fivẹ, mōrẹ, tōẹ ノ e ハ發音セザルコト

（5） ēắch ノ a ハ發音セザルコト

（6） foot ハ單數ニシテ feet ハ複數ナルコト

（7） has ト have トハ同意義ナルモ各其ノ用ヒラル
ル場合ノ異ナルヲ注意記憶スベキコト

讀方ハ

（1） Show⌢me your *hands*ˋ.

（2） How many *fingers have*⌢*you*ˋ?

（3） I have ten fingersˋ.

(109)

(4) Five fingers on the⌢right hand′, and five more on the⌢left‵.

(5) This⌢is my right foot‵.

(6) This⌢is my left foot‵.

(7) My feet have five toes each‵.

(8) Each finger has a⌢nail‵.

(9) Each toe has a⌢nail‵.

(10) Two hands have ten nails‵.

(11) Each foot has five nails‵.

譯解ハ

(1) 汝ノ兩手ヲ余ニ示セ

(2) 汝ハ幾本ノ指ヲ有ツカ

(3) 余ハ十本ノ指ヲ有ツ

(4) 右ノ手ニ五本ノ指又左ノ手ニ尙五本

(5) 是ハ余ノ右足デアル

(6) 是ハ余ノ左足デアル

(7) 余ガ兩足ニハ各五本ノ指ガアル

(8) 手ノ指ニ一枚ヅツノ爪ガアル

(9) 足ノ指ニ一枚宛ノ爪ガアル

(10) 二本ノ手ニ十枚ノ爪ガアル

(11) 孰レノ足ニモ五枚ノ爪ガアル

(110)

5. 十一新語ノ發音及ビ譯解ノ練習ヲナサシメ次ニ
本課十一文章ノ讀方及ビ譯解ヲ練習セシム

6. 綴字

thin, think, thick, thatch, theft, both, pith,
tooth, moth, mouth.

先ヅ是等ノ單語ノ發音ヲ聞キテ綴字ヲナサシメ次ニ
綴字ヲ示シテ發音ヲナサシムベシ

7. 書方

How many fingers have you?
Five fingers on the right hand, and
five more on the left. My feet
have five toes each. Each toe has a
nail.

是等ノ文章ノ讀方及ビ譯解ヲナサシムベシ

讀方ハ

How many *fingers have⌒you`*? Five fingers on
the⌒right hand′, and five more on the⌒left`. My
feet have five toes each`. Each toe has a⌒nail`,

(III)

譯解ハ

汝ハ幾本ノ指ヲ有ツカ、右ノ手ニ五本ノ指又左ノ手
ニ尚五本、余ガ兩足ニ五本宛ノ指ガアル、足ノ指ニ一
枚宛ノ爪ガアル

第 二 十 三 課

I. 復習

păpä′, fŏŏt, thĕm, bŏx, Jŏḥn's ŏf, ẉhọ, yọ$\mathrm{u}$rs,
fēẹt, whȳ, ō′pẹn, wh$\mathrm{a}$t, fāçẹ, gŭn, ēᶏch, quĭtẹ,
nōsẹ, châir, whêrẹ, bĕnch, cȯmẹ, māᶍ, our, thĭngs,
ĭṣn't fôr, ᶏl′sō, bōōts, boys, rīgḥt, ḳnōẉ, new,
pụt, vĕr′ỹ, gīrls, hēr, wē, George, theᶍ, wrĭtẹ,
dōȯr, w$\mathrm{a}$nt, one, twọ, eyes, many, mouthṣ,
Eng′lĭsh, lĕt′tērs, ᶏl′phᶏbĕt, lēᶏth′ēr.

Please show⌒me your fingers`.

How many *fingers have* you on the right hand`?

I have *five* fingers on the⌒right hand`.

How many *feet have*⌒you`?

I have *two* feet`.

(112)

Each foot has five toes', and each toe has five nails`.

rend, slit, cold, chat, wood, stud, split, flake, steed, eschew, drink, gate, plight, town, pair, chair, food, brood, that, these, mouth, thin.

The large letters are called "Capital Letters." Our teachers has a pen, but we have pencils. How many eyes have you? I have two eyes. Who gave you all these things? Papa gave them to me. Five fingers on the right hand, and five more on the left.

2. 實物又ハ圖畫ニヨリ十箇ノ卵ヲ入レタル箱ガ床ノ上ニアルヲ示シナガラ

What do you see on the floor?

ト問ヒ

I see a box.

(113)

ト答ヘ直チニ之ヲ是認シテ

Very well ; and what are there in the box ?

ト問ヒ

There are some eggs in it.

ト答ノ是ニ於ヲ點頭キナガラ

You are right.　Count the eggs.

ト云ヘバ一箇ヅツ卵ヲ數ヘテ

One, two, three, four, five, six, seven, eight, nine, ten.　There are ten eggs.

ト答フ其ノ時箱ノ中ヨリ三箇ノ卵ヲ取出シナガラ

Let me take three eggs out of the box.

ト云ヒ

How many are there now ?

ト問ヘバ

There are seven.

ト答フ。次ニ尚三箇ノ卵ヲ取出サントシテ

If I take three more, how many will be left in the box ?

ト問フ其ノ答ハ

Only four.

斯ノ如クスルコト數回ニ及ビ生徒ヲシテ其ノ大意ヲ

(114)

悟ラシメ更ニ各文章ノ意義ヲ説明シテ此ノ會話ヲ繰返シ次ノ諸點ヲ教フ

(1) flŏŏr, fŏŭr, ōn'lў ノ ō ハ dŏŏr, ōld ノ ō ト同音ナルコト

(2) wĕlļ, ĕggs, sĕ'vĕn, lĕt, lĕft ノ母音ハ yĕs, tĕn ノ母音ト同ジキコト

(3) ĕggs ノ s ヲ z ト發音セズシテ s ノ清音トナスヲ可ナリトスルコト

(4) count, out ノ母音ハ our, proud, down ノ母音ト同ジキコト

(5) three ハ th ノ清音ト r (initial) ト相並ビ其ノ間ニ母音ヲ挿マザルモノナレバ日本人ニ取リテ十分ノ練習ヲ要スルコト

(6) sĭx ノ sĭ ヲ shĭ トナサザル樣注意スルコト

3. 成ルベク多數ノ生徒ヲシテ實物又ハ圖畫ニヨリ本課十一章ノ發音及ビ譯解ヲ試ミシメ若シ誤謬アル時ハ一々丁寧ニ之ヲ訂正ス

4. 次ニ此十一文章ヲ順次黑板ニ書キ反復其ノ讀方及ビ譯解ヲ教ヘ次ノ諸點ヲ説明ス

(1) flŏŏr ヲ flōōr ト讀マザル樣注意スルコト

(2) floor, well, let, will, left, only ノ l ヲ明確ニ發音スルコト

(115)

(3)　four ノ母音ヲ　our ノ母音ノ如クスルコトナク door ノ母音ノ如クナシテ fōur ト讀ムコト

(4)　sĕv'ẹn ノ第二ノ e ハ發音セザルコト

(5)　eight ノ母音ハ they ノ母音ト同ジク gh ハ發音セザルコト

(6)　left ハ「左」ト云フ意ニアラズシテ「殘さる」ト云フ意ナリ

(7)　only ヲ ŏnly ト讀マズシテ ōnly ト發音スルコト

(8)　will ハ未來ノ事ヲ示セルコト

讀方ハ

(1)　What do‿you see on the‿floor`?

(2)　I see a‿box`.

(3)　Very‿well`; and what are‿there in the‿box`?

(4)　There‿are some *eggs in*‿it`.

(5)　You‿are right`. *Count* the‿eggs`.

(6)　One', two', three', four', five', six', seven', eight', nine', ten`. There‿are *ten* eggs`.

(7)　*Let*‿me take three eggs out‿of the‿box`.

(8)　How many are‿there *now*`?

(9)　There‿are *seven*`.

(116)

(10)　If I take three *more'*, how many will⌒be⌒
left in the⌒box`?

(11)　　Only *four`*.

譯解ハ

　(1)　汝ハ床ノ上ニ何ヲ見ルカ

　(2)　余ハ一ノ箱ヲ見ル

　(3)　誠ニ然リ。　シテ箱ノ中ニ何ガアルカ

　(4)　其ノ中ニ多少ノ卵ガアル

　(5)　其ノ通リデアル。　卵ヲ數ヘヨ

　(6)　一ツ、二ツ、三ツ、四ツ、五ツ、六ツ、七ツ、
八ツ、九ツ、十、十箇ノ卵ガアル

　(7)　余ハ箱ノ中ヨリ三箇ノ卵ヲ取リ出サウ

　(8)　今ハ幾箇アルカ

　(9)　七箇アル

　(10)　余若シ尙三箇ヲ取ラバ箱ノ中ニ幾箇殘ルダラ
ウカ

　(11)　唯四箇

　5.　十六新語ノ發音及ビ譯解ノ練習ヲナサシメ次ニ
本課十一文章ノ讀方及ビ譯解ヲ練習セシム

　6.　綴字

　are, arm, bark, card, dark, farm, garb, hard,
large, park, yard.

(117)

先ヅ是等ノ單語ノ發音ヲ聞キテ綴字ヲナサシメ次ニ
綴字ヲ示シテ發音ヲナサシムベシ

7. 書方

One, two, three, four, five, six seven, eight, nine, ten. There are ten eggs in the box. If I take six eggs out of the box, there will be only four eggs left.

是等ノ文章ノ讀方及ビ譯解ヲナサシムベシ

讀方ハ

One´, two´, three´, four´, five´, six´, seven´, eight´,
nine´, ten`. There⌢are ten eggs in the⌢box`. If
I take six eggs out⌢of the⌢box´, there will⌢be
only four eggs left`.

譯解ハ

一ツ、二ツ、三ツ、四ツ、五ツ、六ツ、七ツ、八ツ、
九ツ、十。箱ノ中ニ十箇ノ卵ガアル。余若シ箱ノ中ヨ
リ六箇ノ卵ヲ取リ出サバ唯四箇ノ卵ガ殘ルダラウ。

(118)

第 二 十 四 課

本課ハ第一課ヨリ第二十三課マデニ教ヘタル所ヲ復
習セシムルモノナレバ一字一語又一音タリトモ未ダ記
憶セザルモノアラバ決シテ次課ニ進ムベカラズ

1. 母音　十九箇

先ヅ此ノ十九箇母音ノ練習ヲナシ各母音ヲ含メル單
語ヲ舉ゲシム

2. 子音　二十七箇

先ヅ此ノ二十七箇子音ノ練習ヲナシ各子音ヲ含メル
單語ヲ舉ゲシム

3. 單語　百八十五箇

各單語ノ發音及ビ譯解ヲ練習シ次ニ各單語ヲ含メル
句又ハ文章ヲ舉ゲシム

4. 本課十五文章ノ讀方及ビ譯解ヲ練習シ殊ニ音調
ノ接續及ビ抑揚ニ注意スベシ又成ルベク直譯ノ弊ヲ避
ケテ純良ナル日本文ニ譯スベシ

讀方ハ

(1) Do⌢you not see many eggs⌢on the⌢table'?

(2) Yes', I see seven or⌢eight eggs`.

(3) Show⌢me your fingers`.

(4) This box is made of⌢wood`.

(119)

(5) Have⌢you my boots′?

(6) No`.   *Roy* has your boots.`

(7) *Whose* shoes are these`?

(8) They⌢are *Kate's* shoes`.

(9) Two boys are here′, and three girls are there`,

(10) How many *hands have*⌢you`?

(11) .I have two hands`.

(12) Who *gave* you this paper`?

(13) Our *teacher gave*⌢it to⌢me`.

(14) *Let*⌢me take⌢up five eggs`.

(15) If you take two of⌢them′, how many will⌢ be⌢left in my⌢hand`?

譯解‥

(1) 汝ハてーぶるノ上ニ多數ノ卵ヲ見ナイカ

(2) 然リ余ハ七八箇ノ卵ヲ見ル

(3) 汝ノ手指ヲ余ニ示セ

(4) 此ノ箱ハ木デ出來テ居ル

(5) 汝ハ余ノ長靴ヲ有ツカ

(6) 否、ろいガ汝ノ長靴ヲ有ツ

(7) 是レハ誰ノ靴デアルカ

(120)

(8)　ソレハけいとノ靴デアル

(9)　二人ノ男兒ガ此ノ所ニ居リ又三人ノ女兒ガ彼所ニ居ル

(10)　汝ハ幾本ノ手ヲ有ツカ

(11)　余ハ二本ノ手ヲ有ツ

(12)　誰ガ此ノ紙ヲ汝ニ與ヘタカ

(13)　我等ノ先生ガソレヲ私ニ下サツタ

(14)　余ハ五箇ノ卵ヲ取リ上ゲヨウ

(15)　汝若シ其ノ中ノ二箇ヲ取ルナラバ余ノ手ノ中ニ幾箇殘ルダラウカ

5. 綴字

who, why, what, when, whet, where, which, whim, whose, whom.

先ヅ是等ノ單語ノ發音ヲ聞キテ綴字ヲナサシメ次ニ綴字ヲ示シテ發音ヲナサシムベシ

6. 書方

Show me your fingers. This box is made of wood. I see many eggs on the table. Let me take up

(121)

five of them. How many more do you see on the table?

是等ノ文章ノ讀方及譯解ヲナサシムベシ

讀方ハ

Show⌒me your fingers`.· This box is made of⌒
wood`. I see many eggs on the⌒table`. *Let*⌒me·
take⌒up five of⌒them`. How many more do⌒you
see on the⌒table`?

譯解ハ

汝ノ手指ヲ余ニ示セ。 此ノ箱ハ木デ出來テ居ル。
余ハてーぶるノ上ニ多數ノ卵ヲ見ル。余ハ其ノ中ノ五
箇ヲ取リ上ゲョウ。汝ハてーぶるノ上ニ尚幾箇ヲ見ル
カ。

第 二 十 五 課

1. 復習

(1) What do⌒you see on the⌒table`?

(2) I see some paper and many pencils`.

(3) Please count the⌒pencils`.

(122)

(4) One', two', three', four', five', six', seven', eight', nine', ten'. There are *ten* pencils'.

(5) If I take four of them', how many pencils will be left on the table'?

(6) There will be *six* pencils left'.

(7) Very well'; let me take four more of the pencils'.

(8) How many are there *now*'?

(9) There are *two*'.

(10) Do you see also some inkstands'?

(11) Yes', I *see* them'.

wend, grit, scold, brat, shook, strut, spade, creek, lewd, blink, spright, proud, where, groom, those, thatch, large, garb, whim, whose.

How many eyes have you? I have two eyes. Who gave you all these things? Papa gave them to me. Five fingers on the right hand,

and five more on the left. One, two, three, four, five, six, seven, eight, nine, ten. Let me take up three of them. How many more do you see on the table?

2. 實物又ハ圖畫ニヨリ全級ノ生徒ニ銀ノ懷中時計ヲ示シナガラ

Mary, will you tell us what this is?

ト問ヒめいりニ代リテ

Yes, sir.　It is a watch.

ト答フ其ノ時手眞似ヲ用ヒテ

Is it round or square?

ト問ヒ

It is round.

ト答フ又

Is this a silver watch?

ト問ヒ

Yes, sir.　It is a silver watch.

ト答フ。次ニ

(124)

Henry, did you ever see a watch before?

ト問ヒへんりニ代リテ首ヲ振リナガラ

No, sir.　I never saw one before.

ト答フ夫ヨリ時計ヲ洋服ノかくしノ中ニ入レテ

Where did I put my watch?

ト問ヒ

You put it in your pocket.

ト答フ次ニ時計ヲ書物ノ下ニ置キテ

Where is it now?

ト問ヒ

It is under the book.

ト答フ。斯ノ如クスルコト數回ニ及ビ生徒ヲシテ其ノ
大意ヲ悟ラシメ更ニ各文章ノ意義ヲ説明シテ 此ノ會話
ヲ繰返シ次ノ諸點ヲ教フ

　(1)　Mā'rў, Hĕn'ry ノ ў ハ短音ナレバめ－り－、へ
んり－ト云ハザル樣注意スルコト

　(2)　ŭs, ŭn'dĕr ノ ŭ ハ bŭt, jŭst, mŭst ノ ŭ ト同音ナ
ルコト

　(3)　sĭr ノ ĭr 及ビ sĭl'vĕr, ĕv'ĕr, nĕv'ĕr, ŭn'dĕr ノ ĕr
ハ fĭrst ノ ĭr 及ビ hĕr ノ ĕr ト同音ナルコト

　(4)　wạtch ノ母音ハ whạt ノ ạ 及ビ ŏn ノ ŏ ト同音
ナルコト

(125)

(5)　round ノ母音ハ our, how ノ母音ト同ジキコト

(6)　squâre ノ母音ハ châir ノ母音ト同ジキコト

(7)　befōre ノ bĕ ハびーニアラズべニアラズびナルコト

(8)　saw ハ sō ニアラザルコト

(9)　pŏckĕt ハぽっきッニアラズシテぽっけっt ナルコト

　　3.　成ルベク多數ノ生徒ヲシテ實物又ハ圖畫ニヨリ本課十二文章ノ發音及譯解ヲ試ミシメ若シ誤謬アル時ハ一々丁寧ニ之ヲ訂正ス

　　4.　次ニ此ノ十二文章ヲ順次黑板ニ書キ反復其ノ讀方及ビ譯解ヲ敎ヘ次ノ諸點ヲ説明ス

　　(1)　Mā′ry ハめーありト發音スルヨリモめいりト云フヲ優レリトスルコト

　　(2)　ĭs ノ s ハ濁音 z ニアラズシテ清音ナルコト

　　(3)　squâre ノ qu ヲ k ト同一ニセズシテ kw トナスコト

　　(4)　ĕv′ĕr, nĕv′ĕr ヲ ē′vĕr, nē′vĕr ト讀マザル樣注意スルコト

　　(5)　befōre′ ノ後半 fore ヲ高調ニスルコト

　　(6)　sir ハ鄭重ナル文章ノ中ニ用ヒラルヽコト

　　(7)　Mā′rў, sĭl′vĕr, Hĕn′rў, ĕv′ĕr, nĕv′ĕr, pŏck′ĕt,

(126)

ŭn'dĕr ハ其前半ヲ高調ニスベキコト

讀方ハ

(1) Mary', will⌢you *tell*⌢us what this⌢is' ?

(2) Yes',⌢sir`. It⌢is a⌢*watch*`.

(3) Is⌢it round' or squ ⴝre`?

(4) It⌢is *round*`.

(5) Is this a⌢silver watch' ?

(6) Yes',⌢sir`. It⌢*is* a⌢silver watch`.

(7) Henry', did⌢you ever see a⌢watch before'?

(8) No',⌢sir`. I *never* saw one before`.

(9) Where did⌢I put my watch`?

(10) You *put*⌢it in⌢your *pocket*`.

(11) Where *is*⌢it now`?

(12) It⌢is under the⌢*book*`.

譯解ハ

(1) めいりヨ、汝ハ是ガ何デアルカヲ我等ニ告ゲテ呉レルカ

(2) 然リ君ヨ、ソレハ一箇ノ懷中時計デアル

(3) ソレハ圓形カ方形カ

(4) ソレハ圓形デアル

(5) 是ハ一箇ノ銀時計デアルカ

(127)

(6)　然リ君ヨ、ソレハ一箇ノ銀時計デアル

(7)　へんりヨ、汝ハ是迄一箇ノ懷中時計ヲ見タコトガアルカ

(8)　否君ヨ、余ハ是迄見タコトガナイ

(9)　余ハ何處ニ余ノ懷中時計ヲ置イタカ

(10)　汝ハ汝ノかくしノ中ニソレヲ置イタ

(11)　ソレハ今何處ニアルカ

(12)　ソレハ書物ノ下ニアル

5. 十五新語ノ發音及ビ譯解ノ練習ヲナサシメ次ニ本課十二文章ノ讀方及ビ譯解ヲ練習セシム

6. 綴字

all,　ball,　call,　fall,　gall,　hall,　pall,　tall,　wall,　small.

先ヅ是等ノ單語ノ發音ヲ聞キテ綴字ヲナサシメ次ニ綴字ヲ示シテ發音ヲナサシムベシ

7. 書方

Mary, will you tell us what this is? Yes, sir, it is a silver watch. Where did I put the watch? You

(128)

put it under the book.   Henry never

saw a watch before.

是等ノ文章ノ讀方及ビ譯解ヲナサシムベシ

讀方ハ

Mary′, will⌢you *tell*⌢us what this⌢is′?   Yes′,⌢
sir′, it⌢is a⌢silver watch`.   Where did⌢I *put* the⌢
watch`?   You put⌢it under the⌢*book*.   Henry
never saw a⌢watch before`.

譯解ハ

めいりヨ、汝ハ是ガ何デアルカヲ我等ニ告ゲテ呉レ
ルカ、然リ君ヨ、ソレハ(一箇ノ)銀時計デアル、余ハ
懷中時計ヲ何處ニ置イタカ、汝ハ書物ノ下ニソレヲ置
イタ、へんりハ是迄懷中時計ヲ見タコトガナイ

第 二 十 六 課

I. 復習

Pȧpä, tŏŏt, thĕm, pŏck′ĕt, six, Jŏhn's, ŏf, whọ,
yöụrs, · thrēẹ, whȳ, sĕv′ẹn, wạtch, fāçẹ, ŭn′dĕr,
ẹạch, quitẹ, nōṣẹ, châir, squârẹ, whêrẹ, bĕnch,

(129)

cóme, māy, round, thĭngs, ĭṣn't, fôr, ạl'sŏ, bōͅōts,
boys, eĭġht, ḳnōͅw, new, pụt, vĕr'y̆, sīr, hĕr, wē,
George, theͅy̆, wͅrītͅ§, flōōͅr, sͅạw, one, twͅọ, eyes,
many, mouthͅṣ, fōͅụr, Mā'ry̆, bēfōͅrͅ§', Eng'lĭsh,
lĕt'tērs, ăl'phȧbĕt, lĕͅȧth'ēr.

Wĭll⁀you tell⁀me what⁀your name⁀ĭs'?
Yes', sir`. *Henry* ĭs my⁀name`.
What⁀ĭs thĭs *watch made*⁀of`?
It⁀ĭs made of⁀*sĭlver*`.
Where dĭd⁀you put my⁀*doll*`?
I put⁀ĭt on the⁀bĭg *table* there`.

spend, skip, gold, scrap, good, trust, haste,
sweep, flew, ink, tight, count, there, fool, this,
three, bard, whet, which, gall, hall.

Who gave you all these things?
Papa gave them to me. Five
fingers on the right hand, and five
more on the left. One, two, three,

(130)

four, five, six, seven, eight, nine, ten.
Let me take up three of them. How
many more do you see on the table?
Henry never saw a silver watch
before.

2. 實物又ハ圖畫ニヨリ全級ノ生徒ニ赤色ノ 薔薇花
ヲ示シナガラ

What a beautiful flower it is!

ト云ヒ

Do you know the name of this flower?

ト問ヒタル後生徒ニ代リテ

Yes, sir.　It is a rose.

ト答フ又

Is this a white rose, or a red rose?

ト問ヒ

It is a red rose.

ト答フ次ニ

How do you like the rose?

ト問ヒ

(131)

I like the rose very much.

ト答ヘ次イデ

Mamma likes the rose better than any other flower.

ト云フ。依ツテ其ノ生徒ニ薔薇花ヲ與ヘナガラ

You may take this to your mamma.

ト云ヘバ生徒ハ會釋シナガラ

I am much obliged to you.

ト答フ。最後ニ

Why do you like the rose?

ト問ヘバ

Because it smells so sweet.

ト答フ。斯ノ如クスルコト數回ニ及ビ生徒ヲシテ其ノ大意ヲ悟ラシメ更ニ各文章ノ意義ヲ說明シテ此ノ會話ヲ繰返シ次ノ諸點ヲ敎フ

(1) beau'tiful ノ beau ニ於ケル母音ハ new ノ母音ト同ジキコト

(2) rose ノ母音ハ nose ノ母音ト同ジクろーうzナルコト

(3) white ハ wit ニアラズシテ hwit ナルコト

(4) like ハ「如ク」ノ意ニアラズシテ「好ム」ノ意ナ

ルコト

(5) Mámmä′ ノ後半ヲ高調ニスルコト

(6) ŏblīg′ęd ノ līg ヲ高調ニスルコト及ビ g ト d トノ間ニ母音ヲ挿入セザルコト

(7) bĕcaụ̆sę̆′ ノ ạ ハ all ノ ạ 及ビ fôr ノ ô ト同音ナルコト

(8) swē̆ę̆t ハ s いー t ニアラズシテ s ういー t ナルコト

3. 成ルベク多數ノ生徒ヲシテ實物又ハ圖畫ニヨリ本課十二文章ノ發音及ビ譯解ヲ試ミシメ若シ誤謬アル時ハ一々丁寧ニ之ヲ訂正ス

4. 次ニ此ノ十二文章ヲ順次黑板ニ書キ反復其ノ讀方及ビ譯解ヲ敎ヘ次ノ諸點ヲ説明ス

(1) bę̆ảū′tǐfụl ノ ea ハ發音セザルコト又此ノ如ク長キ語ハ緩々ト發音スベキコト

(2) flower ハ flou＋ĕr ナレドモふらうあトナルニアラズシテふらわトナルコト

(3) mámmä′ ヲまんまート讀マズシテままートスルコト又前半ヲ高調ニスル人モアレドモ後半ヲ高調ニスルヲ正シトスルコト

(4) bĕt′tĕr ハ lĕt′tĕr ニ於ケルガ如クべったート讀マズシテべたート云フベキコト

(133)

(5)　ŏblĭg′ĕd ノ高調節ト ĭ 音トニ注意スベキコト

(6)　bĕcạu̯ṣẹ′ ノ高調節ト be ノ bĕ ニアラズシテ bĕ ナルコトニ注意スベキコト

(7)　I am obliged ハ「負フ所アル」トカ「有リ難ウ」トカ云フ意ナルコト

讀方ハ

(1)　What⌒a⌒*beautiful* flower it⌒is`!

(2)　Do⌒you know the⌒name of this flower′?

(3)　Yes′,⌒sir`.　It⌒is a⌒*rose*`.

(4)　Is this a⌒*white* rose′, or⌒a *red* rose`?

(5)　It⌒is a⌒*red* rose`.

(6)　How do⌒you *like* the⌒rose`?

(7)　I like the⌒rose very *much*`.

(8)　Mamma likes the⌒rose better than any other flower`.

(9)　You may take *this* to⌒your Mamma`.

(10)　I am much⌒*obliged* to⌒you`.

(11)　Why do⌒you *like* the⌒rose`?

(12)　Because it *smells* so⌒sweet`.

譯解ハ

(1)　ソレハ何タル美シキ花デアルカヨ

(134)

(2) 汝ハ此ノ花ノ名ヲ知ルカ

(3) 然リ君ヨ、ソレハ(一輪ノ)薔薇花デアル

(4) 是ハ(一輪ノ)白薔薇花デアルカ又ハ(一輪ノ)赤薔薇花デアルカ

(5) ソレハ(一輪ノ)赤薔薇花デアル

(6) 汝ハ何ノ位薔薇花ヲ好ムカ

(7) 余ハ大ニ薔薇花ヲ好ム

(8) 母ハ他ノ何ノ花ヨリモ薔薇花ヲ好ム

(9) 是ヲ汝ノ母御ノ許ニ持チ行キテ宜シイ

(10) 誠ニ有リ難ウ

(11) 何故汝ハ薔薇花ヲ好ムカ

(12) ソレガアンナニ芳バシク匂フ故ニ

5. 十三新語ノ發音及ビ譯解ノ練習ヲナサシメ次ニ本課十二文章ノ讀方及ビ譯解ヲ練習セシム

6. 綴字

her, fern, germ, jerk, pert, term, verb, sir, bird, dirt, firm, girl.

先ヅ是等ノ單語ノ發音ヲ聞キテ綴字ヲナサシメ次ニ綴字ヲ示シテ發音ヲナサシムベシ

7. 書方

What a beautiful flower it is!

(135)

*How do you like the rose?　I like
the rose better than any other flower.
Why?　Because it smells so sweet.*

是等ノ文章ノ讀方及譯解ヲナサシムベシ

讀方ハ

What⌒a⌒*beautiful* flower it⌒is`! How do⌒you
like the⌒rose`? I like the⌒rose better than any
other flower`. Why`? Because it *smells* so sweet`.

譯解ハ

ソレハ何タル美シキ花デアルカヨ、汝ハ何ノ位薔薇
花ヲ好ムカ、余ハ他ノ何ノ花ヨリモ薔薇花ヲ好ム、何
故カ、ソレガアンナニ芳バシク匂フ故ニ。

————

第 二 十 七 課

1. 復習

Mamma´, fŏot, thăn, sīx, Jŏhn's, ŏf who, yoųrs,
three, whȳ, sĕv´ẹn, wạtch, fāçẹ, mŭch, ēạch,
quītẹ, rōsẹ, châir, squârẹ, whêrẹ, bĕnch, cômẹ,
māy, round, thĭngs, ĭsn't, fôr, ạl sō, boots, boys,

(136)

eîght, knōw, new, put, věr'y̆, sīr, hēr, wē, George,
they, wrīte, flōor, bĕcạuṣe', one, twǫ, eyes, many,
mouths, fōur, flower, bĕt'tēr, ŏblĭgĕd, Mā'ry̆,
bēfōre', Eng'lĭsh, ăl'phăbĕt, lĕăth'ēr, bĕạu'tĭfụl.

What⌒a⌒large table it⌒is`!

How do⌒you like your teacher`?

I like our teacher very *much*`.

Mamma', do⌒you like the⌒rose'?

O' Yes`, I *like*⌒it better than any other flower`.

He⌒is much *obliged* to⌒you`.

trend, grip, scold, flap, hook, drunk, chaste,
street, skew, clink, fright, ground, spare, gloom,
than, thick, hard, white, small, verb, firm.

*Five fingers on the right hand,
and five more on the left. One, two,
three, four, five, six, seven, eight, nine,
ten. Let me take up three of them.
How many more do you see on the*

(137)

*table? Henry never saw a silver
watch before.   I like the rose better
than any other flower, because it smells
so sweet.*

2. 實物又ハ圖畫ニヨリ數箇ノ林檎ヲ入レタル籠ヲ
持テル男兒ヲ全級ノ生徒ニ示シナガラ其ノ男兒ニ向ヒ
テ

Tarō, what have you in the basket?

ト問ヒ其ノ男兒ハ

I have a few apples in it.

ト答フ依ツテ

What are you going to do with them?

ト問ヘバ

I am going to take them to my uncle.

ト答フ尙

Are you going to give him all these apples?

ト問ヒ

Yes, I am.

ト答フ。次ニ實物又ハ圖畫ニヨリ一箇ノ蜜柑ヲ手ニ持
テル女兒ヲ示シナガラ其ノ女兒ニ向ヒテ

(138)

Hana, what have you in the hand?

ト問ヒ其ノ女兒ハ

I have an orange.

ト答フ

Who gave it to you?

ト問ヘバ

My aunt was kind enough to give it to me.

ト答フ。次ニ

Are you going to eat it yourself?

ト問ヘバ首ヲ振リナガラ

No, I am going to give it to my little brother
Jirō.

ト答フ。最後ニ

Isn't Tarō a good boy?

Isn't Hana very kind?

ト云フ。斯ノ如クスルコト數回ニ及ビ生徒ヲシテ其ノ
大意ヲ悟ラシメ更ニ各文章ノ意義ヲ 説明シテ此ノ會話
ヲ繰返シ次ノ諸點ヲ敎フ

   (1) few ノ母音ハ new ノ母音ト同ジキコト

   (2) ăp'ple ノ ă ハ ănd ノ ă ニシテ p ト l ト ノ間ニ
母音ヲ挿入セザルコト

(139)

(3) gō'ĭng ノ gō ハ ga ニアラザルコト

(4) ŭn'clę ノ ŭ ハ ŭp ノ ŭ ニシテ c ト l トノ間ニ母音ヲ挿入セザルコト

(5) gĭvę ノ gĭ ヲ gē ト長ク引カザルコト

(6) wąş ノ ą ハ whąt ノ ą ト同音ナルコト

(7) brŏth'ĕr ノ ó ハ còmę ノ ó ト同ジキコト

3. 成ルベク多數ノ生徒ヲシテ實物又ハ圖畫ニヨリ本課十四文章ノ發音及ビ譯解ヲ試ミシメ若シ誤謬アル時ハ一々丁寧ニ之ヲ訂正ス

4. 次ニ此ノ十四文章ヲ順次黑板ニ書キ反復其ノ讀方及ビ譯解ヲ敎ヘ次ノ諸點ヲ說明ス

(1) Tàrō, Hànà, Jìrō ハ日本人名ノ羅馬字綴ニシテ發音ハ日本語ノたらう、はな、じらうナルコト

(2) bàs'kĕt ノ bàs ヲ băs トナサザル樣注意スルコト

(3) ŏr'ăngę ノ ă ハ ā ト同種類ノ音ナレドモ短ク發音スベキコト

(4) äųnt ヲ ąųnt ト發音セザルコト

(5) wąş ヲ wăş 又ハ wàş 又ハ wŭş トナサザルコト

(6) enough ハ ĭnŭf' ニシテ ĕnŭf' ニアラザルコト

(7) brŏth'ĕr ヲ brŏth'ĕr ト讀マザルコト

(8) bàs'kĕt, ăp'plę, gō'ĭng, ŭn'clę, ŏr'ăngę, brŏth'ĕr

(140)

ハ何レモ其ノ前半ヲ高調ニスルコト

(9) enough', yourself' ハ何レモ其ノ後半ヲ高調ニスルコト

讀方ハ

(1) Tarō, what have⌢you in the⌢basket`?

(2) I have a⌢few *apples* in⌢it`.

(3) What⌢are⌢you going to *do*⌢with⌢them`?

(4) I am going to *take*⌢them to my uncle`.

(5) Are⌢you going to *give*⌢him *all* these apples'?

(6) Yes', I *am*`.

(7) Hana', what have⌢you in the⌢hand`?

(8) I have an⌢*orange*`.

(9) Who *gave*⌢it to⌢you`?

(10) My aunt was *kind*⌢enough to *give*⌢it to⌢me`.

(11) Are⌢you going to eat⌢it *yourself*'?

(12) No', I am going to *give*⌢it to my little brother *Jirō*`.

(13) Isn't Tarō a⌢good boy'?

(14) Isn't Hana very kind'?

(141)

譯解ハ

  (1) 太郎ヨ汝ハ籠ノ中ニ何ヲ有ツカ

  (2) 余ハソノ中ニ數箇ノ林檎ヲ有ツ

  (3) 汝ハソレヲ如何ニシヨウトスルカ

  (4) 余ハ余ノ伯父ノ許ニソレヲ持チ行カウトスル

  (5) 汝ハ是等ノ林檎ヲ悉皆彼ニ與ヘヨウトスルカ

  (6) 然リ其ノ積リ

  (7) 花ヨ汝ハ手ノ中ニ何ヲ有ツカ

  (8) 私ハ(一個ノ)蜜柑ヲ有ツ

  (9) 誰レガ汝ニソレヲ與ヘタカ

  (10) 私ノ伯母ハ親切ニモ私ニソレヲ與ヘタ

  (11) 汝ハ自分デソレヲ食ハウトスルカ

  (12) 否私ハ私ノ小キ弟次郎ニソレヲ與ヘヨウトスル

  (13) 太郎ハ(一ノ)善キ男兒デナイカ

  (14) 花ハ甚ダ親切デナイカ

5. 十八新語ノ發音及ビ譯解ノ練習ヲナサシメ次ニ本課十四文章ノ讀方及ビ譯解ヲ練習セシム

6. 綴字

oil, boil, coil, foil, soil, toil, coin, join, loin, void.

先ヅ是等ノ單語ノ發音ヲ聞キテ綴字ヲナサシメ次ニ綴字ヲ示シテ發音ヲナサシムベシ

(142)

7. 書方

What are you going to do with these apples? I am going to take them to my uncle. My aunt was kind enough to give me this orange. Are you going to eat it yourself? O, no!

是等ノ文章ノ讀方及ビ譯解ヲナサシムベシ

讀方ハ

What⌒are⌒you going to *do*⌒with these apples`?
I am going to *take*⌒them to my uncle`.　My aunt was *kind*⌒enough to *give*⌒me this orange`.　Are⌒you going to eat⌒it *yourself*'?　O', no`!

譯解ハ

汝ハ是等ノ林檎ヲ如何ニショウトスルカ、余ハ余ガ伯父ノ許ニソレヲ持チ行カウトスル、余ガ伯父ハ親切ニモ余ニ此蜜柑ヲ與ヘタ、汝ハ自分デソレヲ食ハウトスルカ、イーヤ。

(143)

第 二 十 八 課

1. 復習

Mȧmmä', fŏŏt, thăn, sĭx, Jŏḫn's, ŏf, ẉhọ, yọ̇ụrsĕlf',

thrēḝ, whȳ, sĕv'ḙn, wạ̣ṣ, fāçḝ, ŭnclḙ, ēạt, quitḙ,

rōṣḝ, châir, squârḙ, whêrḙ,, bĕnch, brȯthēr, māẙ,

round, thĭngs, ĭṣn't, fôr, ŏr'ȧnġḙ,, bōōts, boys,

ḙĭgḫt, ḵnōẇ, few, pụt, vĕr'ẙ, sĭr, hēr, wē, Gḙorġḙ,

theẙ, ẇritḙ, flōȯr, flower, ăp'plḙ, äụnt, enough',

ȯblĭġ'ḙd, Mā'rẙ, bēfōrḙ', Eng'lĭsh, ăl'phȧbĕt, léạ̣th'ēr,

bḙạ̇ū'tīfụl, bȧs'kĕt.

What do⌢you find in the⌢basket`?

I find a⌢few *eggs* in⌢it`.

Are⌢you going to *take* them to your⌢aunt'?

Yes', I *am*`.

My brother Tarō was *kind*⌢enough to give me
the⌢apples`.

Isn't⌢he a⌢very good boy'?

went, brisk, bolt, grand, wool, punch, taste;
greet, stew, pinch, wight, hound stare, spoon,

(144)

leather, both, lard, whose, stall, term, mirth, join, toil.

One, two, three, four, five, six, seven, eight, nine, ten. Let me take up three of them. How many more do you see on the table? Henry never saw a silver watch before. I like the rose better than any other flower, because it smells so sweet. My aunt was kind enough to give me this orange.

2. 學校建物ノ側ニ男兒ト女兒ト相語ル圖ヲ全級ノ生徒ニ示シ其ノ女兒ニ代リテ

Good morning, Charles.

ト云ヒ又其ノ男兒ニ代リテ

Good morning, Lucy.

ト云フ其ノ時女兒ハ

Where have you been?

ト問ヒ男兒ハ

(145)

I have been out in the play-ground.

ト答フ又女兒

Were there many boys and girls there?

ト問ヘバ男兒ハ

Yes, there were.

ト答フ而シテ女兒ハ

I was in the house this morning and did not play.

ト云フ。次ニ運動場ニ於テ二三ノ男兒ガ走ル圖ヲ示シナガラ

Let us go out and play.

ト云ヒ

All right.

ト答フ乃チ男兒等運動場ニ出デテ走ル。甲ハ乙ニ向ヒ

How fast you run!

You run very fast.

I can not run so fast as you do.

ト云ヒ遂ニ疲勞ノ樣子ヲ示シテ

I am tired.

ト云フ依ッテ

Let us go into the house.

ト云フ此時一人ノ男兒ハ他ノ男兒ニ向ヒ

I see your sister there.

ト云フ。斯ノ如クスルコト數回ニ及ビ生徒ヲシテ其ノ大意ヲ悟ラシメ更ニ各文章ノ意義ヲ説明シテ此ノ會話ヲ繰返シ次ノ諸點ヲ敎フ

(1) môrn′ĭng ノ môrn ヲ mōrn ト發音セザル樣注意スルコト

(2) Lū′çў ノ Lū ヲ Lōō トナサザル樣注意スルコト

(3) wĕrᶒ ノ母音ハ hĕr, sĭr ノ母音ト同ジキコト

(4) fȧst ノ母音ハ bȧs′kĕt ノ前半ニ於ケル母音ト同ジキコト

(5) rŭn ノ母音ハ bŭt, gŭn ノ母音ト同ジキコト

(6) sĭs′tĕr ノ前半ヲ shĭs トナサザルコト

3. 成ルベク多數ノ生徒ヲシテ圖畵ヲ用ヒテ本課十五文章ノ發音及ビ譯解ヲ試ミシメ若シ誤謬アルトキハ一々丁寧ニ之ヲ訂正ス

4. 次ニ此ノ十五文章ヲ順次黒板ニ書キ反復其ノ讀方及ビ譯解ヲ敎ヘ次ノ諸點ヲ説明ス

(1) Chärlᶒs ヲ Chärlĕs ト讀マザル樣注意スルコト

(2) been ハ bēn ヨリモ寧ロ bĭn ナルコト

(3) plāy′-ground ノ如ク二箇ノ名詞ヲ連結シテ一箇ノ名詞トナスモノハ第一ノ名詞ヲ高調ニスルコト

(147)

(4) wĕr̩ ハ wâr ヨリモ寧ロ wĕr ナルベキコト

(5) ĭn'tǫ ノ後半ニ於ケル母音ハ ōō ナルコト

(6) môrn'ĭng, Lū'çў, ĭn'tǫ, sĭs'tĕr ハ何レモ其ノ前半ヲ高調ニスルコト

(7) morning, Charles, play-ground, house, fast, tired ノ末尾ニ母音ヲ加ヘザルコト

(8) good morning ハ通常「オ早ウ」ト譯シテ可ナレドモ元來午前中ニ用フル挨拶ノ語ナレバ十一時又ハ十二時頃ニ用フル時ハ「オ早ウ」ト云フヨリモ寧ロ「今日ハ」ト譯スベキコト

(9) have been ハ「ツイ今迄居ッタ」ト云フ意ナルコト

(10) was ハ過去ノ單數ニシテ were ハ過去ノ複數ナルコト

讀方ハ

(1) Good *morning*, Charles`.

(2) Good *morning*, Lucy`.

(3) Where have⁀you *been*`?

(4) I have been⁀*out* in the⁀*play*-ground`.

(5) Were there many boys and girls there'?

(6) Yes, there were`.

(148)

(7) I was in the⌒house this⌒morning´, and did not play`.

(8) *Let*⌒us go⌒*out* and play`.

(9) All *right*`.

(10) How *fast* you run`!

(11) You run very *fast*`.

(12) I can not run so⌒*fast* as⌒*you* do`.

(13) I am *tired*`.

(14) *Let*⌒us go into the⌒house`.

(15) I see your *sister* there`.

譯解ハ

(1) ちゃーるすサンオ早ウ

(2) りゅーしサンオ早ウ

(3) 汝ハ何處ニ居タカ

(4) 余ハ運動場ニ出テ居タ

(5) 彼處ニ多數ノ男女兒ガ居タカ

(6) 然リ居タ

(7) 私ハ今朝家ノ中ニ居テ遊バナカッタ

(8) サア外ニ出テ遊ビマセウ

(9) 宜シイ

(10) 何ト速ニ汝ガ走ルヨ

（149）

(11) 汝ハ甚ダ速ニ走ル

(12) 余ハ汝ノ如クソンナニ速ニ走ルコトガ出來ヌ

(13) 余ハ疲レタ

(14) サア家ノ中ニ入リマセウ

(15) 余ハ彼處ニ汝ノ妹(又ハ姉)ヲ見ル

5. 十三新語ノ發音及ビ譯解ノ練習ヲナサシメ次ニ
本課十五文章ノ讀方及ビ譯解ヲ練習セシム

6. 綴 字

ask, bask, cask, mask, task, cast, fast, last,
mast, past, vast, gasp.

先ヅ是等ノ單語ノ發音ヲ聞キテ綴字ヲナサシメ次ニ
綴字ヲ示シテ發音ヲナサシムベシ

7. 書 方

Good morning, Charles. Where have you been? I have been out in the play-ground. I was in the house and did not play. I can not run so fast as you do.

是等ノ文章ノ讀方及ビ譯解ヲナサシムベシ

(150)

讀方ハ

Good *morning*, Charles`. Where have⌒you been`? I have been⌒*out* in the⌒*play*-ground`. I was in the⌒house′ and did not play`. I can not run so⌒*fast* as⌒*you* do`.

譯解ハ

ちゃーるすサン オ早ウ。 汝ハ何處ニ居タカ。 余ハ運動場ニ出テ居タ。 私ハ家ノ中ニ居テ遊バナカッタ。余ハ汝ノ如クソンナニ速ニ走ルコトガ出來ヌ。

────────

第 二 十 九 課

1. 復 習

fȧst, fŏŏt, thăn, sĭx, Jŏhn's, ŏf, whǫ, yǫụrsĕlf′, thrēē̦, whȳ, sĕv′ęn, wạs, Lu′çy̆. ŭn′clę, ēạt, quītę, rōṣę, châir, squârę, whêrę, bench, brŏthĕr, thĭngs, ĭṣn't, môrn′ĭng, ŏr′ăngę, bōots, boys, eịght, knōw, few, pụt, vĕr′y̆, sȋr, wē, wērę, George, theỵ, wrītę, flōǫr, flōw′ēr, ăp′plę, äụnt, Chärlęs, been, enough′, ŏblĭg′ęd, Mā′ry̆, bĕfōrę′, Eng′lĭsh, ăl′phȧbĕt, lĕạth′ēr, bĕạū′tĭfụl, bȧs′kĕt, plāỵ-grounḑ.

(151)

Good *morning*⸜.   Have⌒you been in the⌒play
ground′ ?

No⸜.   I have been in the⌒*house*⸜.

Was there my sister Lucy′ ?

No⸜.   I did not *see*⌒her⸜.

Do you run very fast′ ?

No⸜.   I can not run so⌒*fast* as⌒*you* do⸜.

spend, strict, sold, span, shook, stump, snake,
speed, blew, sphinx, slight, mound, spare, swoon,
that, thick, Charles, why, pall, were, birch, broil,
flask, vast.

Let me take up three of them.
How many more do you see on the
table? Henry never saw a silver
watch before. I like the rose better
than any other flower, because it smells
so sweet. My aunt was kind

(152)

enough to give me this orange. Good morning, Charles. Have you been out in the play-ground?

2. 大人ト生徒ト對話ノ圖ヲ全級ノ生徒ニ示シ先ヅ大人ニ代リテ生徒ニ向ヒ

What is the name of your teacher?

ト問ヒ生徒ニ代リテ

Mr. Nishimura is his name.

ト答フ

How long have you been learning English?

ト問ヘバ

I have been learning English for a year.

ト答フ

What have you been reading?

ト問ヘバ

I have been reading the First Reader.

ト答フ

When will you finish it?

ト問ヘバ

(153)

I shall finish it next week.

ト答フ次ニ

How old are you?

ト問ヘバ

I am eleven years old.

ト答フ

John is twelve, is he not?

ト云ヘバ

Yes, he is a year older than I am.

ト應ヘ又

I am two years younger than Mary.

ト云フ故ニ大人ハ

Then, Mary is thirteen years old.

ト云ヒ更ニ

How many letters are there in the English alphabet?

ト問ヘバ生徒ハ

There are twenty six letters in the English alphabet.

ト答フ。斯ノ如クスルコト數回ニ及ビ生徒ヲシテ其ノ大意ヲ悟ラシメ更ニ各文章ノ意義ヲ説明シテ此ノ會

（154）

話ヲ繰返シ次ノ諸點ヲ數フ

(1) lĕȧrn'ing ノ前半 lĕarn ニ於ケル母音ハ hĕr, wẽrȩ ノ母音ト同ジキコト

(2) yēȧr ハ cȧr ノ前ニ y ノ音ヲ冠ラセタルモノナルコト

(3) yȯŭng'ĕr ノ前半 yȯŭng ニ於ケル母音ハ bŭt, gŭn ノ母音ト同ジキコト

(4) thĭr'tēȩn ノ前半 thĭr ニ於ケル母音ハ sĭr, fĭrst ノ母音ト同ジキコト

3. 成ルベク多數ノ生徒ヲシテ圖畫ニヨリ本課十六文章ノ發音及ビ譯解ヲ試ミシメ若シ誤謬アル時ハ一々丁寧ニ之ヲ訂正ス

4. 次ニ此ノ十六字文章ヲ順次黑板ニ書キ反復其ノ讀方及ビ譯解ヲ教ヘ次ノ諸點ヲ説明ス

(1) Mr. ハ Mĭs'tĕr ノ略字ニシテ最初ノ M ト最後ノ r トヲ並べ書キタルモノナレバ發音ハ矢張 Mĭs'tĕr ナルコト

(2) Mr. ノ終ニ付シタル period (.) ハ略字ノ符號ナルコト

(3) lŏng ノ ng ハ鼻音ナルコト

(4) shăll ヲ shȧll ト發音セザル樣注意スルコト

(5) ēlĕv'ȩn ノ最初ノ c ヲč ト發音セザルコト又其

(155)

ノ高調節ニ注意スルコト

(6) twĕlvḙ ノ t ト w トノ間、l ト v トノ間、又 v ノ後ニ母音ヲ入レザル樣注意スベキコト

(7) Mĭs′tĕr, lĕạrn′ĭng, fĭn′ĭsh, ōld′ĕr, yǫŭng′ĕr, thĭr′tēḙn, twĕn′tў ノ前半ヲ高調ニスルコト

(8) will, shall ハ未來ニ屬スルコトヲ述ブル時ニ用ヒラルヽコト又兩者ノ區別ニモ着目スベキコト

讀方ハ

(1) What⌒is the⌒*name* of⌒your teacher`?

(2) Mr. *Nishimura* is his name`.

(3) How *long* have⌒you been learning English`?

(4) I have been learning English for⌒a⌒year`.

(5) What have⌒you been reading`?

(6) I have been reading the⌒First Reader`.

(7) When will⌒you *finish*⌒it`?

(8) I shall *finish*⌒it next *week*`.

(9) How *old* are⌒you`?

(10) I am eleven years old`.

(11) John⌒is *twelve*′, is⌒he not`?

(12) Yes′, he⌒is a⌒year *older* than *I*⌒am`.

(156)

(13) I am two⌒years *younger* than Mary`.

(14) Then, Mary is *thirteen* years old`.

(15) How many *letters* are⌒there in the⌒ English *alphabet*`?

(16) There⌒are twenty six letters in the⌒ English *alphabet*`.

譯解ハ

(1) 汝ノ先生ノ名ハ何デアルカ

(2) 其ノ名ハ西村サンデアル

(3) 汝ハドノ位長イ間英語ヲ學ンダカ

(4) 余ハ一年間英語ヲ學ンダ

(5) 汝ハ何ヲ讀ンダカ

(6) 余ハ第一讀本ヲ讀ンダ

(7) 汝ハ何時ソレヲ終ラウトスルカ

(8) 余ハ次ノ週ニソレヲ終ラウトスル

(9) 汝ハ幾歳デアルカ

(10) 余ハ十一デアル

(11) じょんハ十二歳デアル──デナイカ

(12) 然リ彼ハ余ヨリモ一歳年長ケテ居ル

(13) 余ハめーりヨリモ二歳若クアル

(14) 然ラバめーりハ十三歳デアル

(15)　英語ノあるふぁべっと二幾箇ノ文字ガアルカ

(16)　英語ノあるふぁべっと二二十六箇ノ文字ガアル

5.　十六新語ノ發音及ビ譯解ノ練習ヲナサシメ次二本課十六文章ノ讀方及ビ譯解ヲ練習セシム

6.　綴字

bay, day, gay, hay, lay, may, pay, ray, say, way, clay, gray, play, slay, stay, tray,

先ヅ是等ノ單語ノ發音ヲ聞キテ綴字ヲナサシメ次二綴字ヲ示シテ發音ヲナサシムベシ

7.　書方

I have been learning English for a year. We have just finished the First Reader. John is twelve years old, is he not? Yes, he is a year older than I am. There are twenty six letters in the English alphabet.

是等ノ文章ノ讀方及ビ譯解ヲナサシムベシ

讀方ハ

I have been learning English for⌒a⌒year`.

(158)

We have *just*⌢finished the⌢First Reader`.

John⌢is twelve years old′, is⌢he not`?

Yes′, he⌢is a⌢year *older* than I⌢am`.

There⌢are twenty six letters in the⌢English *alphabet*`.

譯解ハ

余ハ一年間英語ヲ學ンダ。我等ハ丁度第一讀本ヲ終ッタ。 じょんハ十二歳デアル――デナイカ。 然リ彼ハ余ヨリモ一歳年長ケテ居ル。 英語ノあるふぁべっとニ二十六箇ノ文字ガアル。

─────────

第 三 十 課

本課ハ本卷第一課ヨリ第二十九課マデニ敎ヘタル所ヲ復習セシムルモノニテ 一字一韻又ハ一音タリトモ未ダ記憶シ得ザル者アラバ決シテ次卷ニ進ムベカラズ

1. 單語　二百六十箇

各單語ノ發音及ビ譯解ヲ練習シ次ニ 各單語ヲ含メル句又ハ文章ヲ擧ゲシム

2. 本課二十文章ノ讀方及ビ譯解ヲ 練習シ殊ニ音調ノ接續及ビ抑揚ニ注意スベシ又成ルベク 直譯ノ弊ヲ避ケテ純良ナル日本文ニ譯スベシ

(159)

讀方ハ

(1) Where did⌒you put that silver watch`?

(2) I *put*⌒it in my⌒*pocket*`.

(3) Did⌒you ever read an⌒English book'?

(4) Yes', I have *just*⌒finished the⌒First Reader`.

(5) Will⌒you take some of⌒these *apples'*?

(6) *Thank*⌒you very⌒*much*`.

(7) Do⌒you know the⌒name of⌒this *flower'*?

(8) Yes', I *know*`. It⌒is a⌒*rose*`.

(9) How many *eggs are*⌐there`?

(10) There⌒are *eight* eggs`.

(11) Put six of⌒them in this *box*`.

(12) *Let*⌒us go⌒*out* to the⌒*play*-ground`.

(13) I can *not* go⌒*out* to⌒play`.

(14) You may go into the⌒*house* now`.

(15) Whose shoes are⌒these`?

(16) They⌒are Mary's shoes`.

(17) These shoes are very *large'*, are⌒they not`?

(18) How many *letters* are⌒there in the⌒ English *alphabet*`?

(160)

(19) There⌒are twenty six`.

(20) Very *well*`. You may take your seat`.

譯解ハ

(1) 汝ハアノ銀時計ヲ何處ニ置イタカ

(2) 余ハ余ノかくしニソレヲ置イタ

(3) 汝ハ是迄英書ヲ讀ンダコトガアルカ

(4) 然リ余ハ丁度第一讀本ヲ終ツタ

(5) アナタ是等ノ林檎ヲ少々オ取リナサイ

(6) 誠ニ有リ難ウ

(7) 汝ハ此ノ花ノ名ヲ知ツテ居ルカ

(8) 然リ余ハ知ツテ居ル、ソレハ(一ノ)薔薇花デアル

(9) 幾箇ノ卵ガアルカ

(10) 八箇ノ卵ガアル

(11) 其ノ六箇ヲ此ノ箱ニ入レヨ

(12) サア運動場ヘ出テ行カウ

(13) 余ハ遊ビニ出テ行クコトガ出來ナイ

(14) 汝ハ最早家ノ中ニ入ツテモ宜シイ

(15) 是ハ誰ノ半靴デアルカ

(16) ソレハめーりノ半靴デアル

(17) 此ノ半靴ハ甚ダ大キイ——デナイカ

(18) 英語ノあるふぁべっとニ幾箇ノ文字ガアルカ

(19) 二十六アル

(161)

(20)　誠ニ然リ。　汝ノ坐ニ著イテ可ナリ

3. 綴 字

nether, tether, leather, feather, weather, whether, gather, rather, bother, mother, brother.

　先ヅ是等ノ單語ノ發音ヲ聞キテ綴字ヲナサシメ次ニ
綴字ヲ示シテ發音ヲナサシムベシ

4. 書 方

Tarō is two years older than Jirō.
Mary is three younger than Charles.
Henry has a basket of apples. Lucy
is going to eat an orange. Papa
and Mamma are so fond of roses.
They are good and kind to me.

　是等ノ文章ノ讀方及ビ譯解ヲナサシムベシ
讀方ハ

Tarō is two years *older* than Jirō`.　Mary is
three years *younger* than Charles`.　Henry has a⌒
basket of⌒*apples*`.　Lucy is going to⌒eat an⌒

(162)

orange`.　Papa and Mamma are so⌒fond of⌒*roses*`.
They are good and *kind* to⌒*me*`.

譯解ハ

　太郎ハ次郎ヨリモ二歳年長ケテ居ル。　めーりハちゃーるすヨリモ三歳若イ。　へんりハ一籠ノ林檎ヲ有ツ。りゅーしハ一箇ノ蜜柑ヲ食ハウトスル。　父上及ビ母上ハ大層薔薇花ガ好キデアル。　彼等ハ余ニ對シテ善イ親切ナ人デアル

明治四十二年十一月十六日印刷
明治四十二年十一月十九日發行
明治四十三年四月二十日再版發行

定價金貳拾五錢

著作權者　　文　部　省

　　　　　　東京市日本橋區新右衞門町十六番地
發　行　者　株式會社國定教科書共同販賣所

　　　　　代表者　大　橋　新　太　郎

　　　　　　東京市牛込區市ヶ谷加賀町一丁目十二番地
印　刷　者　飯　田　三　千　太　郎

　　　　　　東京市牛込區市ヶ谷加賀町一丁目十二番地
印　刷　所　株式會社秀英舍第一工場

發　行　所　株式會社國定教科書共同販賣所
　　　　　　東京市日本橋區新右衞門町十六番地

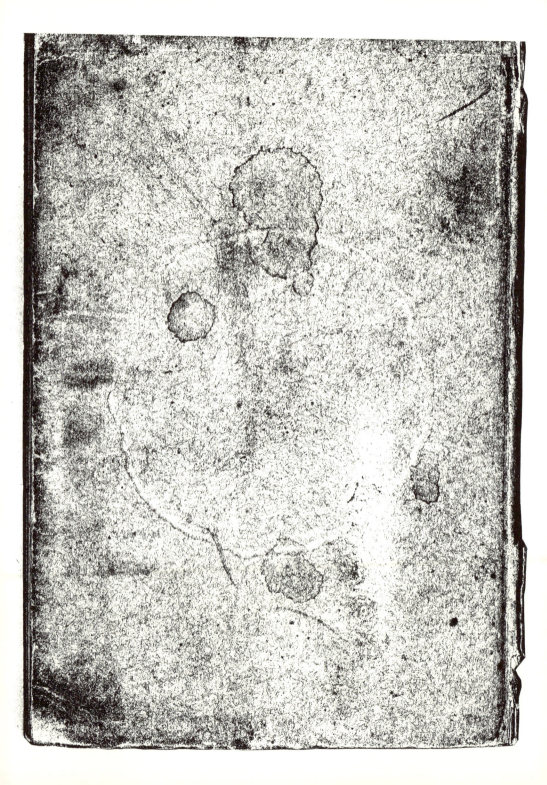

解　題

江利川 春雄
（和歌山大学教育学部教授・日本英語教育史学会会長）

解 題

文部省 *The Mombushō English Readers for Elementary Schools*
（小学校用文部省英語読本）
全3巻、1908〜10（明治41〜43）年

　この国定教科書は文部省著作としては初めての高等小学校専用の英語読本
で、発行は株式会社国定教科書共同販売所だったが、1930（昭和5）年10月1
日以降は大日本図書株式会社による「文部省許可譲授発行」となった。全3巻
で、第1巻は1908（明治41）年3月19日発行、本文は全30課81ページ＋ロー
マ字表3ページ。第2巻は1909（明治42）年3月30日発行、目次2ページ＋本
文30課120ページ＋単語リスト8ページ。第3巻は1910（明治43）年4月23日
発行、本文30課66ページ＋単語リスト15ページである。いずれの巻も、週
2時間程度の授業時間数を想定して編纂されている。

　この小学校用文部省英語読本は、実に30年以上にわたって使われ続けた。
そのため、戦前期の小学校英語教育史および英語教科書史において重要な位
置を占める教科書である。また、その教師用指導書は、文部省当局がどのよ
うな小学校英語教育を進めようとしていたのかを知るための最重要資料であ
る。

高等小学校の発足と英語教育
　小学校の外国語教育（実質は英語教育）は明治初期にさかのぼるが、本格的
に実施されるようになったのは、欧化主義政策下の1884（明治17）年に改正さ
れた小学校教則綱領で「英語の初歩を加ふるときは読方、会話、習字、作文
等を授くべし」と規定されてからである。なお、本解題では、原文の旧漢字
は新漢字に、送り仮名のカタカナはひらがなに改めた。

　1886（明治19）年には、4年制の義務教育機関だった尋常小学校に接続する
4年制の高等小学校制度（学齢10〜13歳）が発足した。当初は大半の高等小学
校が加設科目（学校選択科目）として英語を教えた。だが、すぐに激しい英語

I

廃止論に見舞われ、数年後には英語教育の実施校が激減した（江利川2017）。

明治33（1900）年8月の第3次小学校令では、高等小学校は2年制～4年制となり、英語を加設できるのは4年制課程に限るとされた。改正された小学校令施行規則によれば、英語科の教授方針は「綴字」より始まる旧来型から「発音」から始める音声重視の導入法へと改善されている。

英語は簡易なる会話を為し、又近易なる文章を理解するを得しめ、処世に資するを以て要旨とす／英語は発音より始め、進みて単語、短句及近易なる文章の読み方、書き方、綴方並に話し方を授くべし

英語の文章は純正なるものを選び、其の事項は児童の智識程度に伴ひ、趣味に富むものたるべし／英語を授くるには常に実用を主とし、又発音に注意し、正しき国語を以て訳解せしめんことを努むべし

1907（明治40）年3月21日の小学校令改正によって、翌年度から義務教育が6年制に延長され、尋常小学校から直接中学校に進学できるようになった。高等小学校は2年制（一部は3年制）となり、入学年齢は中学生と同じながら一段劣る初等教育機関とされ、卒業後は就職することを前提とする完成教育機関となった。復刻した『小学校用文部省英語読本』と教師用指導書は、この時期に刊行されたものである。

その後、高等小学校の英語教育はさまざまな変遷を遂げつつ、戦後の新制中学校が発足する直前の1946（昭和21）年度まで約60年間続けられた。英語を課した小学校は都市部が中心で、女子よりも男子が多く履修し、ピーク時の1932（昭和7）年度には全国で1,842校（全体の9.9%）の高等小学校が英語を課していた（江利川2006、233ページ）。

文部省著作英語読本の系譜

文部省著作の英語教科書は、すでに1887（明治20）年に中等学校用の *English*

Readers: High School Series（全6巻）と1889（明治22）年発行の *The Mombushō Conversational Readers*『正則文部省英語読本』（全5巻）が作られている。

　検定教科書制度が発足した1886（明治19）年から国定期に移行する1905（明治38）年までに、民間が発行する文部省検定済の小学校用英語教科書は64種類あった（江利川2006）。しかし、1904（明治37）年度以降の小学校用教科書は原則として文部省著作による国定と定められた。そのため、文部省は外国語学校（東京外国語大学の前身）の教授だった浅田栄次に委嘱し、初めての高等小学校用英語教科書である *The Mombushō English Readers for Elementary Schools*（『小学校用文部省英語読本』）を1908（明治41）年から3年間に毎年1冊ずつ刊行した。

　ただし、1908（明治41）年改訂の小学校令施行規則によれば、英語科に関しては必ずしも文部省著作の教科書を使用する義務はなかった。にもかかわらず、1907（明治40）年から1921（大正10）年までは新規の検定認可を受けたのは英習字練習帳のみであり、民間の手になる検定英語読本は一切発行されなかったから、この期間の高等小学校は文部省英語読本だけによる国定教科書時代となった。

　こうして、『小学校用文部省英語読本』は1939（昭和14）年に第1巻の新版が出るまで、誤植訂正と軽微な修正はあるものの、実に30年以上にわたって使用され続けた。その間の総発行部数を『文部省年報』の各年版から計算すると、約244万部にも達する。最高は1921（大正10）年度の19万6千冊、最低は1929（昭和4）年度の5千冊と変動が激しく、平均すると毎年約8万冊である。ただし、当時は中古の教科書が譲渡されていたため、実際の英語学習人口はこの数字よりも多い。

　文部省は明治末期の旧版に代わり、1939（昭和14）年にようやく *The New Monbusyō English Readers for Elementary Schools*（全2巻）の刊行を開始した。発行所は大日本図書株式会社で、第1巻が1939（昭和14）年7月26日発行、1941（昭和16）年2月10日訂正発行（改訂部分はごくわずか）、同年2月12日文部省検

査済。第2巻は1941（昭和16）年2月26日発行および文部省検査済。奥付の和文タイトルは「文部省英語読本」（ただし文部省第67年報では「文部省小学新英語読本」）である。この教科書は第2巻まで出そろった段階で、1941（昭和16）年4月に小学校が改称されて発足した国民学校高等科用の国定英語教科書となった。

新教科書は、その名前とは裏腹に、内容的には明治の旧版との継承性はなく、全く新しい著作である。巻一では本課（70ページ：25課）に先だって4ページにわたる Introductory Sound Drill（口頭練習）が付き、オーラル・メソッドの影響がわかる。

この国定教科書の巻一が半分ほどに縮約され、敗戦1年前の1944（昭和19）年9月に文部省著作の『高等科英語』（全1巻）として刊行された。総ページ数は60ページ、本文はわずか30ページで、この1冊が「一二年生用」とあるから、せいぜい週1時間程度の授業を想定していたと思われる。

『高等科英語』は敗戦直後に改訂され、1946（昭和21）年度の暫定教科書として1年だけ使用された。第1分冊は1946（昭和21）年2月20日翻刻発行、第2分冊は5月17日文部省検査済、8月30日翻刻発行である。このように、『高等科英語』は、準義務教育的な大衆教育機関であった高等小学校・国民学校高等科においても、英語科教育が戦中戦後を通じて連続的に行われていたことを証明している。こうした蓄積が、新制中学校の英語教育に活かされるのである。

浅田栄次について

今回復刻した『小学校用文部省英語読本』の編纂の中心となった浅田栄次（あさだ・えいじ　1865〜1914）は、山口県徳山に生まれ、帝国大学理科大学数学科を1年で中退して渡米した。神学と言語学を修め、シカゴ大学で第1号となる博士号を取得して1893（明治26）年に帰国し、青山学院神学部教授を経て、1897（明治30）年より東京の外国語学校英語科主任教授となった。

1902（明治35）年には文部省から教科書調査委員を命じられ、1907（明治40）年には神田乃武や岡倉由三郎らと共に中等学校に於ける英語教授法調査委員、翌1908年から11年にかけて文部省視学委員を努めるなど、文部省との関係が深かった。『小学校用文部省英語読本』とその教師用指導書の執筆に加え、中学校用の英語教科書も編纂するなど英語教育界に大きな足跡を残したが、外国語学校教授だった1914（大正3）年に49歳で急逝した。浅田栄次の業績と人間像は、浅田みか子夫人の編集になる大著『浅田栄次追懐録』（私家版、1916）に集大成されている。

『小学校用文部省英語読本』の編纂方針

『小学校用文部省英語読本』の編纂事情に関しては、当時の文部省図書局長を務めた渡部薫之介が「故浅田栄次君に就きて」（浅田1916、570〜571ページ）で次のように述べている（句読点補充）。

初め第一巻編纂前、編纂方針に関して東京帝国大学文科大学教授文学博士中島力造君、東京女子高等師範学校教授黒田定治君の二君、及び余と共に審議決定の上〔浅田栄次が〕編纂に着手せられ、脱稿するや東京外国語学校教師英人オースチン・ウイリアム・メッドレー氏の校閲を経て本省に提出あり、遂に刊行するに至りたり。第一巻と第二巻とに含める挿絵は東京美術学校教授岡田三郎助君、同じく習字用艸体文字〔筆記体〕は池原遠君の筆に成るものなり。各巻世に行はれたる後多少の誤植等あり、是亦常に浅田君を煩はして訂正刊行したるものにして、高等小学校の英語教科書として実際全国唯一のものなり。

ここで述べられている編纂方針に関しては、浅田栄次が文部省用の罫紙2葉に書き残した「高等小学校用英語教科書編纂方針」が、山口県徳山市立図書館所蔵「浅田栄次関係資料」に残されている。幸い、竹中龍範教授（香川大

学）から筆写資料を提供されたので、以下に紹介したい。なお、九から十一までと十三の後半は朱線で抹消されたため割愛した。

　　　　高等小学校用英語教科書編纂方針
　　　　　全体に関するもの
一、文章は総て会話体となし小学校に於ける英語教授の本旨に従ふ

二、徹頭徹尾帰納的教授を用ふ

三、材料は実際的にして我邦の児童に対して適切なるものを択ぶ

四、本邦人に取りて簡易なる字音より始め徐々と困難なる字音に進む

五、発音は概してウェブスター大辞典に依り其符号を用ふ

六、簡易普通の語句より漸次難渋なる語句に移る

七、文法も亦簡単なるものより漸次複雑なるものに進む

八、文法は特に文法として教へず文章より帰納的に之を学ばしむ

十二、先づ客観的語句を教へ而して後主観的語句を教ふ

十三、各巻三十課を置き一課を教ふるに凡二時間即ち一週間を要すべき予
　　　定なり

　　　　　第一巻に関するもの
一、殆ど全く教場内又は学校内に於て実物教授をなし得べき材料を取る

二、第七課より綴字の練習をなさしむ但し既知の語に類するものを集めて
　　之を示す

三、第一巻に於てアルファベット全部の実例を示し且つ大字と小字とを　悉
　　皆学び得しむ

四、習字の練習も第一巻に於てアルファベット全部の大字及小字を学び得
　　しむるの組織なり

五、アルファベットを巻首に載せず帰納的に文字を教へて第一巻の終に至
　　り既知の文字を並列してアルファベットの表を作り之を示す

六、英語中十九種の母音二十七種の子音悉皆第一巻の中にあり

七、最初はペン、インキ、等英語の儘にて日本語に入りたる語を教へ漸次難渋なる語に移る

八、第一巻に載せたる名詞は概ね単数にして仮令複数あるも不規則なる形なし

九、 第一巻に載せたる働詞〔＝動詞〕は主として現在の形のみ

十、 第一巻中の文章は殆ど皆短文なり

十一、パンクチュエーションの符号中最も普通なるものは第一巻に於て之を教ふ

十二、五課を卒る毎に練習課を置く

十三、日本語の羅馬字綴を省く

十四、国文英訳の練習を省く

　以上の方針のもとに編纂された教科書を見てみよう。言語材料では、新語数が第1巻265、第2巻382、第3巻539の合計1,186語。これは2008年に改訂された中学校学習指導要領の語彙1,200語程度とほぼ同じだが、時間数が半分（週2時間）だったことを考えると、現在よりもハードだった。

　文法項目に関しては、編纂方針に「簡単なるものより漸次複雑なるものに進む」とあるものの、実際は多くの項目が総花的に散りばめられている。第1巻には、現行の中学校2年生以上の教科書に配当されている重文、第4文型（SVOO）、未来形、受身、比較、不定詞、現在完了、第5文型（SVOC）、複文、現在完了進行形なども含まれている。第2巻には付加疑問、仮定法、関係代名詞などが盛り込まれている。現在の感覚では、入門期のテキストとしては教えにくく、児童にもかなりの負担を課す教材だと見なせよう。しかし、文法統制がまだ不十分だった明治末期においては、この文部省英語読本の文法配列が特に劣っていたわけではない。

　この国定英語教科書および教師用指導書に対しては、刊行当初から斎藤

（1909）、長井（1910）などによって「旧式である」等の厳しい批判も寄せられた。その詳細については江利川（1992）を参照されたい。

文部省英語読本を使った教案例

　愛媛県師範学校の教諭であった杢田與惣之助（1882〜1960、第3巻の解題参照）は、1908（明治41）年に『小学校用文部省英語読本』（1908）巻一第13課の教案（指導案）を書き残している。筆者はこの教案の全文を江利川（1992、2014）で覆刻したので、ここでは教案に現れた教授法の特徴について概略を述べるにとどめる。

　①音声指導を重視し、会話主体の授業である。

　②本やペンなどの実物を教具として使い、頻繁に「動作にて示す」という
　　指示を与えることで、和訳を排している。

　③英語のみを使う直接教授法（Direct Method）に基づいて授業を進めており、
　　教案の最後は「意味は邦語の媒介なくして了解し得」という総括で締め
　　くくくられている。

文部省『小学校用文部省英語読本巻一教授書』文部省、
　　1909（明治42）年

　小学校の教員は道府県立の師範学校（明治末期は4年制）を卒業することが原則だったが、その師範学校では英語が週3時間程度で、英語教授法に関しては最終学年で合計5時間程度を当てるのが精一杯だった。また、正規の教員免許を持たない代用教員も少なくなかった。そのため、小学校の教員は一般に英語力、英語指導力ともに乏しかった。

　そうした事情から、文部省は教師の英語指導を支援するために『小学校用文部省英語読本巻一教授書』を1909（明治42）年11月19日に発行した。緒言

1ページ＋本文162ページの懇切丁寧な指導マニュアルである。

この教授書の成立事情についても、文部省の渡部薫之介が前述の「故浅田栄次君に就きて」（571ページ）で次のように述べている。

小学校に於ては英語教師の知識最も不十分なれば、少くとも巻一に関し教師用参考書の編纂を必要とすとの議あり。是亦浅田君の独力起草に成り、小学校用文部省英語読本巻一教授書と題し、明治四十二年十一月十九日に刊行せられ、其発行部数今日〔1915年度〕迄四万八千冊に達せりと云ふ。

『小学校用文部省英語読本巻一教授書』は、緒言で教師に対する8ヶ条の注意事項を述べている。

1．毎課の教授に先だち組織的教案を作り細密なる順序を定むべし
2．教師の発音は明瞭正確なるを要す
3．実物又は図画を用ひて教授すべし。図画を用ふる際は読本中の挿絵と均しき掛図を用ふるを可とす
4．教授の際初は生徒に耳に由りて学ばしめ次に口を以て練習せしめ其の次に目を以て講読せしめ最後に手を以て書き綴らしむ。この順序に従ふは極めて肝要にして教課を教ふるの際決して初より読本を開かしむべからず
5．新課の初に必ず既修の諸課に就きて復習せしむべし
6．復習課に於ては既修の諸課を漏なく復習せしむべし
7．毎課の教授に要する時間は凡そ二時間たるべし
8．生徒学力の程度又は時間の分量等により教師は臨機の変化をなすべし

このように、教師は授業に先立って必ず教案を作成し、発音に気をつけ、実物や図画を効果的に活用し、文字に入る前に音声指導を徹底すること、復習

9

を重ねて反復練習を行わせることなどを盛り込んでいる。いずれも、妥当な方針である。ただし、実際の学校現場で、この方針通りの指導が行われたかどうかについては疑わしい（後述）。

この指導書が刊行された明治末期には、民間の検定教科書のための優れた教師用指導書も出ていた。たとえば、『小学校用文部省英語読本巻一教授書』の３年前に刊行された田中虎雄（東京府師範学校教諭）の『井上小学英語読本教授書　第一巻』（金港堂書籍、1906）は、冒頭で小学校英語科教授法の批判と改革の提言を詳述している。その中の「小学校の英語教授に伴へる各種の弊」（児童数の過多、時間数の僅少、英語教員の実力不足、ローマ字教授の弊害、訳読主義の弊害、必修科から随意科へ）では、第２次小学校令（1900）の規定について、「実に立派な目的であるが実際にはこの目的の十分の一も達せられていないのである。或は四年間にやっと神田氏の改訂前の小学英語読本の一巻だけ教へたとか或は〔平易に〕改正した神田読本の第二巻までしか出来ませんとか云ふ学校も往々ある」と現場の実状を述べている。

また小学校英語の教授法についても、「近年小学校の各科教授法は長足の進歩をして随分立派な成績をあげられた所のあるのに英語科のみは尚 甚 幼稚な状態にあるのは遺憾千万なことである」と憂えている。その上で、①小学教育における英語の理想とこれを実現する方法（低学年は耳の練習、高学年は朗読が一番大切）、③教授法詳論（発音、読み方、翻訳、文法、書取、会話）、④Preliminary Lessons（読本に入る前に３ヶ月かけて音声等の練習）を提起している。

明治30年代には英語教授法改革運動が高まりをみせ、小学校の英語科教授法に関しても上記のような優れた方針が提起されていた。文部省の『小学校用文部省英語読本巻一教授書』も、こうした研究と実践の上に執筆されたのである。

2020（平成32）年度から小学校高学年で外国語（英語）が教科化されるいま、文部省が小学校用に刊行した英語読本と教師用指導書から学ぶ意義は大きい。

参考文献

浅田みか子編（1916）『浅田栄次追懐録』私家版（復刻版は東京外語会有志により1996年）

江利川春雄（1992）「小学校用国定英語教科書の成立と変遷」神戸大学大学院教育学研究科
英語教育研究会『KELT』第8号

江利川春雄（2006）『近代日本の英語科教育史：職業系諸学校による英語教育の大衆化過程』
東信堂

江利川春雄（2008）『日本人は英語をどう学んできたか：英語教育の社会文化史』研究社

江利川春雄（2010～2014）「明治期の小学校英語教授法研究：杢田與惣之助『英語教授法綱要』
の翻刻と考察（1～5）」『和歌山大学教育学部紀要・人文科学』第60～64号

江利川春雄（2017）「小学校英語教育の是非をめぐる戦前期の論争」日本英語教育史学会第
33回全国大会（福島大会）口頭発表資料

斎藤大蔵（1909）「国定小学校英語読本を評す」『教育学術界』第19巻第6号、1909（明治
42）年9月10日号

長井氏晁（1910）「文部省著小学英語読本教授書に就いて」『教育時論』第892号、1910（明
治43）年1月25日号

英語教育史重要文献集成　第1巻
小学校英語

2017年9月20日　初版印刷
2017年9月25日　初版発行

監修・解題　江利川 春雄

発 行 者　荒井秀夫

発 行 所　株式会社 ゆまに書房
　　　　　　東京都千代田区内神田 2-7-6
　　　　　　郵便番号　101-0047
　　　　　　電　話　03-5296-0491（代表）

印　　刷　株式会社 平河工業社

製　　本　東和製本 株式会社

定価：本体19,000円＋税

ISBN978-4-8433-5292-2 C3382

落丁・乱丁本はお取替えします。